Alexander Pushkin:
Master Teacher of Dance

by **GENNADY ALBERT**

With a foreword by
MIKHAIL BARYSHNIKOV

Translated by Antonina W. Bouis

The New York Public Library

*Aleksandr Pushkin. Shkola Klassischeskogo Tants*a was originally published in 1996 by Actor. Producer. Theater, Moscow.

Russian text copyright © 1996 by Gennady Albert
English translation © 2001 by Baryshnikov Productions, Inc.
Foreword © 2001 by Mikhail Baryshnikov
All rights reserved

The name "The New York Public Library" and the representation of the lion appearing in this work are registered marks and the property of The New York Public Library, Astor, Lenox and Tilden Foundations.

Library of Congress Cataloging-in-Publication Data

Al'bert, G. (Gennadii)
    [Aleksandr Pushkin. English]
    Alexander Pushkin : master teacher of dance / by Gennady Albert ; translated by Antonina W. Bouis ; with an introduction by Mikhail Baryshnikov.
       p. cm.
    Includes bibliographical references.
    ISBN 0–87104–452–8 (hard : alk. paper)
       1. Pushkin, Aleksandr, (Aleksandr Ivanovich), 1907–1970. 2. Dance teachers--Russia (Federation). 3. Ballet--Study and teaching--Russia (Federation)--Saint Petersburg--History--20th century.

GV1785.P87 A813 2001
792.8′028′092--dc21
[B]   2001041049

First published in English in 2001 by
The New York Public Library
Publications Office
476 Fifth Avenue
New York, NY 10018
www.nypl.org

Printed on acid-free paper
Printed and bound in the United States
Designed by Kara Van Woerden

Acknowledgments

The author wishes to thank the students, colleagues, and close friends of Alexander Ivanovich Pushkin, without whose help this book could not have been written, especially: Valeria Chistyakova, initiator and inspiration of this monograph; Mikhail Baryshnikov, first reader of the book and author of its foreword; Alla Bor, guardian of the unbreakable bonds between us, the students, and our teacher.

The New York Public Library gratefully acknowledges the generous support of the Rudolf Nureyev Dance Foundation, which made possible the publication of this book.

The Dance Division is grateful for the continued guidance and encouragement of Robert Gottlieb.

Contents

vi	Foreword: To the Reader *Mikhail Baryshnikov*
2	**Ballet Soloist** Chapter 1
36	**Legacy** Chapter 2
70	**Teacher** Chapter 3
108	**Pushkin's School** Chapter 4
165	Notes
171	Appendix: *A. I. Pushkin's Classes*
190	About the Jerome Robbins Dance Division

Foreword: To the Reader

The publication of this book elicits in every student of Alexander Ivanovich Pushkin a wave of infinitely tender memories of this amazing man. We owe him so much for what he contributed to that most important period of our formation as dancers.

I think that this publication is an event for the entire ballet world. This is not only a monograph about a brilliant teacher of dance and a handbook for professionals of the choreographic stage. It is also, and perhaps most importantly, a serious attempt to examine the development of the school of Russian ballet from the perspective of the entire century. This book is a great help in understanding the consecutive development of ballet pedagogy from Petipa and his comrades-in-arms Johansson and Cecchetti through the line of brilliant names such as Legat, Obukhov, and Ponomarev, to the master pedagogue, Pushkin, who perhaps without knowing it embodied and crystallized the best ideas of the most important European schools of choreography. He did not blindly re-create the exercises and skills of his great predecessors but intuitively transformed them in relation to the evolution of the art of ballet.

More than a quarter century has passed since Alexander Ivanovich's death, and nearly a decade since the death of his most famous graduate, Rudolf Nureyev. Teacher and student believed in each other and in the end opened the door to immortality for each other. And the great number of Pushkin's students now working in ballet theaters all over the world—dancers, teachers, choreographers—are the best memorial to their teacher. I am pleased to note that this book about our mentor and the glorious traditions of Russian ballet instruction is written by a student of Alexander Pushkin.

A few words about the book as a manual. The three Pushkin classes included are no more than an example of the harmony and wholeness of his educational assignments. They are the fruit of priceless experience, but not the solution to all problems, since Pushkin worked with every class, with all his students, for several years, determining fully the course of their formation, both professionally and as human beings.

His pedagogy did not turn into a rigid, regimented system, like that of some of his outstanding contemporaries. However, he may have done more than anyone else to preserve the purity of connections to his predecessors, to the past of Russian and world ballet. It is this that gave his creative views a breadth and freedom that were not typical of his generation. He regarded with interest various schools of modern choreography, and he could take delight in the crystalline dancing and artistry of Erik Bruhn, the feline softness and plasticity of the young Jean-Pierre Bonnefous, and the innovative productions of various choreographers.

Finally, a wish. The reader should not be put off by the book's special ballet terminology and concrete descriptions of classical steps—they are easy to step around. What you have here is an enjoyable and accessible book—a book about a teacher and his students, written by a not-indifferent author. Everything that it conveys about bringing up a ballet artist applies to other spheres of life and art. In essence, this is a book about raising and educating individuals and about the work of a great artist and teacher.

Mikhail Baryshnikov

Alexander Pushkin:
Master Teacher of Dance

Ballet Soloist

CHAPTER 1

Please accept among the students of the school entrusted to you my brother, Alexander Pushkin, age 15.
Semyon Ivanovich Pushkin. March 31, 1923.[1]

Appoint Alexander Ivanovich Pushkin as of February 5 as instructor of classic dance in the evening division.
Excerpt from Order No. 20 to the Leningrad State Choreographic Technicum, dated February 5, 1932.[2]

Dry lines from an application and an excerpt from an official order, but behind them lies the fate of an artist and master teacher. The beginnings of two careers. One ended after twenty-seven years on the stage. The second lives on in his students, many of whom traveled far—some scattered by the Soviet creative roadblock—throughout the world. Some students recall the past with joy; others feel a never-ending ache. When you find yourself on the truly St. Petersburgian and majestic Architect Rossi Street, once called Theater Street, you unconsciously look for features from the past. And they are there.

I feel I must confess straight off: I never saw Alexander Ivanovich Pushkin dance. But my memory stubbornly retrieves one day in 1967....

A ballet studio of the Agrippina Yakovlevna Vaganova Choreographic School. Softly, as if afraid of scaring off listeners, the piano played. Two students, a young girl and boy, stood near the barre and watched the dancers closely, with some surprise. The dancers, humming along with the melody, were doing the adagio from the ballet *Le Pavillon d'Armide*, to the music of Nikolai Tcherepnin.

When the melody ended (it was finished by the piano alone: the dancers didn't have enough breath left to complete it), silence reigned in the classroom for an instant. "All right, now we'll teach," the teacher concluded—perhaps angrily, perhaps guiltily. The students were uncomfortable at having inadvertently spied upon their elders and their secret—the secret of the eternal thirst for dance.

The teachers were Lidia Tuntina and Alexander Pushkin. They had forgotten their ages, the presence of their students, and were dancing—not at full strength, of course—the adagio from *Armide*. Eyes, arms, and bodies lived in the duet. There were no lifts—only promenades on the floor; there were no pirouettes on toes, but the ideal positions of partners during the turns were demonstrated; there were no tiny steps on toe or airy leaps, but there was something more important: the manner, the line of movement, the perception of the essence of what was being performed. This was not a dance lesson but a lesson through dance: "This is how you must dance and how you must find the ability to give yourself up to dance."

A bit wearily, the teacher went over to the mirror and, as if trying to find a reflection of more than the room itself, stood there silently for a long time. Perhaps it was in this very room that, forty-two years earlier, he had rehearsed for his graduation performance in *The Brook*, newly choreographed by the instructor of the men's class, Vladimir Ponomarev (Vaganova had helped choreograph some of the variations). The male lead was being danced by graduating student Alexander Pushkin.

Behind him were years of study, and the years when he and his brother, Semyon, would run to watch performances at the Palace Theater in Petrograd and sometimes actually got to be in the crowd scenes. Their parents were not interested in the arts. Their father, a peasant from Tverskaya Province (where his son Alexander was born in 1907, in the village of Mikulino) who had moved to St. Petersburg, worked as a lathe operator in railroad shops, while the mother brought up the children. His older brother's love of theater influenced ten-year-old Sasha, but

The Pushkin family: Alexander Pushkin (standing, far right); his brother, Semyon Pushkin (standing, center).

he took another path in art. Semyon, however, remained true to dramatic theater and committed his life to Petrograd's Theater for the Young Viewer, which was founded in 1922 by Alexander Briantsev. From there he volunteered for World War II and died defending his native Leningrad. After the war, Leonid Makaryev, who had also been involved in founding the children's theater, wrote a play called *Sergeant Pushkin*, dedicated to the life of the actor-soldier. Alexander Pushkin seldom spoke of his older brother, but he kept the letters and postcards Semyon sent from theater tours around the country. To Sasha, his older brother was a model of loyalty to art and to the principle of total focus on whatever you do.

Twelve-year-old Sasha wrote in his diary: "I would die if I were deprived of the pleasure of watching ballet." And then, "My dream is the ballet. On March 16 my heart stopped waiting, and I went to find out how to get into ballet school."[3] But Pushkin was not accepted at the Petrograd Theater School: he was too old. That left the School of Russian Ballet under the Baltic Fleet, where they took overaged students. The school, at number 6, Pochtamtskaya Street, was organized and headed by the famous critic and philosopher Akim Volinsky, who worshipped ballet and felt the need for a serious school to prepare artists for classical ballet. At the School of Russian Ballet, Pushkin was taught by faithful custodians of classical dance: Natalia Nikolayeva (wife and partner of Nikolai Legat), Alexander Chekrygin, and L. N. Pavlova. Legat himself came to the classes. "N. Legat and A. Volynsky came to two lessons," Pushkin recorded. "I think they really liked how we work." Agrippina Vaganova also taught there, but she did not stay long: in 1921 she was hired by the Petrograd Theater School. A year later, Legat and Nikolayeva left their homeland forever. Before his departure, Legat wrote to Volynsky that he was not satisfied with working with overaged students; he didn't like having to explain the ABCs to grown people. So the "temple of Terpsichore" collapsed.... But that was later, three years later, and in 1919 Pushkin eagerly awaited the start of his studies. At last, his first class, his first movement at the barre. And he was always upset if a lesson was cancelled because Nikolayeva was busy. Every lesson was a holiday for Pushkin the student, and it remained that way for Pushkin the teacher.

The school on Architect Rossi Street maintained its hold on his imagination, and so in the summer of 1921 he began taking Vaganova's classes. "In the summer I studied for a month and a half with Agrippina Yakovlevna Vaganova," his diary reads. "She was very pleased personally and sent me to the theater school, where I went—but they did not take me." Failure once again. But that did not diminish Sasha's persistence. His studies with the superb teachers Vaganova and Chekrygin laid a solid foundation for his mastery of classical dance.

In March of 1923, his dream came true at last. The minutes of the board meeting of the State Academic Theater School record: "In view of Doctor L. F. Brunner's report on A. Pushkin's suitability in terms of health to enter the school, as well as the conclusion of the instructors of special subjects about his perfectly acceptable level of preparation, accept Alexander Pushkin as a student in the Ballet Department of the School."[4] And so began a new stage in his studies, the studies that would define his teaching style. He spent two years in the class of the marvelous teacher Vladimir Ivanovich Ponomarev. And then came April 12, 1925.

The critic Yuri Brodersen wrote, "... there hasn't been this kind of success for a long time in the graduation performances."[5] "The graduation performance of the Academic Ballet School brought everyone who truly loves the art of choreography much joy; we haven't seen such an interestingly performed and extraordinarily well done school production in a long time,"[6] echoed another reviewer.

The interest in the graduates was justified. Just the name Marina Semenova, who danced the role of the fairy Naila in *La Source*, the three-act ballet by Léo Delibes and Leon Minkus, explains the praise. The critics recognized the talent and training of the young dancers, but then went on to ponder the state of contemporary ballet, striking a note of concern—for the future of the new generation and, of course, for the general situation in ballet. The critics' evaluations of the graduates' work involved issues that were agitating ballet criticism of the 1920s:

The graduation performance of La Source, *choreographed with talent by V. Ponomarev in accordance with all the rules of the true, grand classical ballet, is imbued with solo and ensemble dancing scenes, cleverly designed and often brilliantly executed. Nevertheless, objectivity and impartiality demand that I acknowledge that* La Source *is primarily a dance picture and least of all pantomime, that fundamental dramatic linchpin. And this "pushing" the dance part of the performance at the expense of the dramatic context, at the expense of the pantomime, is the main flaw not only of this graduation performance but of all our ballet theater.*[7]

That was the opinion of several of the critics. And yet the sumptuous halls of the former imperial theaters were already filled with new audiences. Despite anticipated hostility to classical ballet, these audiences understood and came to love *The Sleeping Beauty* and *Swan Lake*. The following lines from the June 1926 issue of *Rabochii i teatr* [Worker and the Theater] were appropriate: "The question of the future existence of choreographic theater is absolutely tied to the new audience. The successful choreographer will be the one who takes into account the laws of social movement on the one hand and the new psychology on the other." Of course, taking the laws of social movement into account was essential, but it was also important that the new audiences

Alexander Pushkin in his graduating class.

Alexander Pushkin, graduate of the Theater School.

Alexander Pushkin (back row, center) with members of the graduating class.

accept ballet's classical legacy. Some critics and choreographers failed to see that and created an artificial barrier between the past and the present of ballet.

Naturally, the plot of *The Brook*, with its fairy Naila, hunter Dzhamil, and gypsy Morgab, was remote from the interests of the new audience, especially since the few pantomime scenes explaining the plot development were not performed very well: "Semenova is primarily a dancer; as an actress she is significantly weaker—lacking still a sharply defined individuality, with rather colorless mimicry.... Pushkin is a strong, agile partner and a not-bad classical dancer; but his exaggerated affectation and naive mimicry create a pathetic impression,"[8] noted a perhaps too severe critic. Even so, the ballet pleased the audience, who had come to love the purity of classical dance, and the dancers received many flattering comments, also:

Semenova's dancing is breath-taking, which is unusual. Of the other student performers, the most remarkable were Berg the First and Pushkin, strong enough to be considered fully mature for responsible performances in the academic ballet theater.[9]

Graduates Pushkin and Kavokin both partnered the ballerina successfully; the former was the better dancer and the latter supported the ballerina more confidently.[10]

It should be noted that all the reviewers mentioned Pushkin's solid preparation as a dancer, singling him out from among the graduates in the men's class. Yet his acting abilities were not persuasive. Of course, the dancers were young and couldn't handle the technical difficulties as well as the acting, but it's important to remember that each critic perceived the young graduates through the prism of his own understanding of the needs of contemporary ballet.

Thus, since Abashidze felt that ballet had

to reflect Noverre's commandments and subsume dance to pantomime and expressive gestures, he found that "the performers all suffer from wan and inexpressive gestures and weakly developed mimicry."[11] Gvozdev, in an article devoted to Semenova, expressed regret that her art might well revive the past but not find for itself a worthy place in the future.

Gvozdev was not a bad prophet. While Pushkin did dance in contemporary ballets, Semenova danced in very few new works in the 1920s, 1930s, and 1940s. Her sphere remained the classic ballets of the past, where her artistry was truly unique. But "the future" that Gvozdev foresaw didn't triumph in the 1930s and 1940s.

Paradoxically, the distancing of Pushkin, Semenova, and other adherents of "pure" classical dance from the new tendencies in ballet allowed them to solidify the foundation that classical dance so sorely needed in the 1950s and 1960s. It was dancers like them, who had preserved the traditions of the ballet, who would raise a new generation that brought contemporary Russian ballet to a higher level of accomplishment. The creative life of Pushkin the performer may have been spent in a narrow track, but it was a bridge to the broader road of his students. And Semenova's brilliant mastery helped give birth to a new, dynamic and expressive performing style that was to further develop the traditions of Russian choreographic art.

What was going on in the ballet theater that Pushkin joined after his graduation performance? Why did reviewers use every opportunity to talk about the situation of contemporary choreography?

We know that trends in the theater are not born in an instant, and that every step in the development of any art is measured in years; this is especially true of choreography. And each of these steps is conditioned by the preceding stages.

Of course, the historical era was so extraordinary that it left a powerful imprint on the development of ballet. The 1920s were a period of creativity and destruction, error and discovery, an internal logical development and an external chaos of seeking and striving. For "Leftist" art, they were years of experimentation and search. The formation of a clearly expressed direction in modern ballet came only a decade later. In the early 1920s, you could see Fyodor Lopukhov's *The Magnificence of the Universe*, set to Beethoven's Fourth Symphony, on a ballet stage in Petrograd and, at nearby theaters, Petipa's *The Sleeping Beauty*, methodically restored by Lopukhov, and Fokine's ballets *Egyptian Nights* and *Le Pavillon d'Armide*. In Moscow, alongside the experiments of Nikolai Foregger, Lev Lukin, and other adherents of "free dance," who proclaimed that a different kind of dance— "from physical culture," "from the joy of a healthy human body"—was the only true response to the times, there were performances from the Studio of Dramballet. After one of these performances, Victor Iving noted wittily, "Dramballet is a drama that has befallen ballet. The dramballet troupe hasn't yet learned to act, and they already seem to have forgotten how to dance."[12] Also taking place were the improvisations of Isadora Duncan to the music of the *Internationale* and the talented work of choreographer Kasyan Goleizovsky with the Chamber Ballet.

Striving, seeking, questing! That chaos of ideas, views, and aesthetic directions made it hard for young people to find their way. And it was hardest of all for those who could not imagine themselves without classical dance. Alexander Pushkin, faithful graduate of the Academic Theater School, responded only to it. Later, when he was an experienced performer, he would stress that you had to approach the stage image through daily classical lessons, the basis of choreographic art. But then, taught by the extraordinary Vladimir Ponomarev, Pushkin joined the Leningrad

Academic Theater of Opera and Ballet, whose ballet director at that time was Fyodor Lopukhov.

The first few years of working in the theater passed for Pushkin as they did for the majority of talented young dancers. On the one hand, he had a steady place in the corps de ballet; on the other, he was soon given the very complex "peasant pas de deux" in Act I of *Giselle*. The posters show that he danced the *Giselle* pas de deux on March 21, 1926, and on March 27 the shepherd in Act II of Gluck's opera *Orpheus and Eurydice*. In his early years onstage, he danced almost all the pastorales. In fact, he didn't miss a single performance of *The Queen of Spades*, in which he was the constant shepherd in Act II. In his very first season, he was brought into the classical grand pas of *Raymonda*, and the next year was marked by his participation in the wedding dance in *Coppélia*.

Despite the numerous corps de ballet roles performed by Pushkin in his first five years in the theater (waltz and mazurka in *Eugene Onegin*, first dance in *La Bayadère*, dances in *Aida*, and so on), he was never a standard corps de ballet performer. Not every graduate is assigned the "peasant pas de deux" in his very first year. The technical difficulties of that duet make it a kind of benchmark against which future leading classical dancers are measured.

Pushkin had mastered the varied supports that are the foundation of this duet. It is difficult to begin the tours with grand plié in coordination with a partner after a leaping entrance, but Pushkin was an agile partner and helped the ballerina confidently. There are almost no lifts, just one jeté entrelacé on the partner's shoulder. The most difficult part for the dancer is in the variation and first coda. The variation is built on tours en l'air with a fixed fifth position after landing in the first part and pas de bourrée with a soft ballonné skimming across the floor in the second. Pushkin was particularly successful in the "small" and "medium" jumps: a soft plié, elasticity, and a high instep helped him. His positions showed an ideal purity, and in this variation it is particularly important to be able to land in an exact fifth position after the tours en l'air. In the coda, his jumps were particularly fine. In the first part, he did not do the cabriole in the effacée position, as many dancers do, but executed the jump after bringing his foot into a forward effacée. This is a very difficult step, and a dancer needs perfect coordination to do it elegantly and correctly. In the last part, Pushkin moved forward quickly, executing sissonne ouverte battu in the attitude croisée. The extension was deep and the landing very brief, followed immediately by another leap. Pushkin did not do many pirouettes at the end of the variations, but his three or four pirouettes ended in an instant stop.

After the performance on March 21, 1926, the young dancer was to dance less frequently with the corps de ballet. Looking through the programs from the start of the 1925–26 season until 1930, one is surprised by how rarely Pushkin appears. They didn't save him for the big roles, but they didn't "overdance" him in the corps, either. He appeared as the Snow Youth in Lopukhov's *The Ice Maiden* in April 1927, and in March 1928 as Prince Charming in *The Sleeping Beauty*. Certainly Pushkin did not dance a great deal at the start of his creative path, which is a pity, since the early years for any artist are a search for his individuality, his self. Unfortunately, for some ballet dancers the question of individuality and manner is decided while they are still in school. Or rather, it is predetermined.

And it seems that Pushkin's stage life was indeed predetermined within the school. A year before graduation, he danced Colin in *La Fille Mal Gardée* with his constant school partner, Semenova. A reviewer of this production mentioned only the technical side of the dancing, saying nothing about the acting: "Student Pushkin in the role of Colin is a technically strong dancer and not bad partner."[13]

Alexander Pushkin as Prince Charming in *The Sleeping Beauty*.

Nina Zheleznova as Princess Florina, and Alexander Pushkin as the Blue Bird, in the pas de deux from *The Sleeping Beauty*.

The restrained praise for the student and then for the graduate is basically just. He didn't have extraordinary professional gifts or impressive looks. He was not very handsome, in fact. His kind, rather strange face did not have stage quality. Aware of this, he concentrated his efforts in a different direction. Well-proportioned, with an astonishingly soft landing after leaps, and a mastery of jumps, he could cleanly execute the most complicated variations. He devoted himself to mastering classical dance, and this was noted and appreciated both in school and at the theater.

It was only in *The Red Poppy* (1929), after four years with the theater, that Pushkin performed a choreographic number that differed fundamentally from his usual repertoire, and it is interesting that while his previous performances had not attracted the critics' attention, this unusual departure garnered good reviews. The well-known critic and theater historian S. S. Mokulsky wrote: "Of the variety numbers, the novelty dances by Bazarova and Pushkin were excellent in Acts I and III, especially 'The Eccentric and the Ass' in Act I, in which the bravura style of a variety stage divertissement could truly be glimpsed."[14] Here is Bazarova's description of the dance from *The Red Poppy*: "A novelty number, choreographed by Lopukhov in the first act—'The Eccentric and the Ass'—belonged in the comic-amusing class. It was built on acrobatic lifts, various kinds of cartwheels and somersaults. It had a simple plot: The eccentric, which I danced, tried to force his donkey—which Pushkin played with incomparable humor—to amaze the audience with various steps. The ass refused and stubbornly resisted the will of his trainer. Pushkin's gentle and friendly humor helped him a lot in this number."[15]

How did it happen that this dancer, who was not distinguished by acting ability and who, moreover, was without experience in novelty numbers, suddenly did so well? It would be incorrect to attribute this success solely to the fact that his capabilities had not been fully exploited in the early years. Later, in the mid-1930s, acting parts (for instance, the role of the Conductor in the ballet *Lost Illusions*) appeared in Pushkin's repertoire, but they weren't successes for him. In *The Red Poppy* it was the production, Lopukhov's innovations, and the dancer's natural creative energies that determined his success. However, to push the young dancer still further would have required weightier means: the ability to transform himself was simply not in Pushkin's nature. He was more interested in strictness of form and an abstract ideal of classical dance. And this was not merely an interest in the virtuoso side of performance: flawlessly obeying the rules of the proper execution of classic steps, Pushkin did not try to complicate their technical level. He was no virtuoso; rather, he sought the path to exact and perfect execution. His interpretation of a step was the quintessential tour en l'air, assemblé, jeté, and so on. This demanded exacting work. Every morning at the classic technique lesson he could be seen checking every pose, the approach to every movement....

  In the diary Pushkin kept in his school years, we find entries such as this one: "Worked on double tours. When will I be able to do them cleanly?" Even then, Pushkin the teacher was being formed. He depended throughout his entire life on classical dance, and his loyalty to it would eventually bring him world fame, not as a dancer but as a teacher. The explanation for that is both simple and complicated. The talents of a performer and those of a teacher differ. Pushkin was a gifted dancer, but he was an outstanding teacher. Accustomed to searching for the path to total mastery of the technique for executing every step, he was able to transfer his experience to others. Dancing many of the most difficult variations in the classical repertoire, he discovered methods for training the body so that it would obey the dancer's will.

  The start of Pushkin's work in the theater

coincided with the establishment of Soviet ballet. The second half of the 1920s was a time of heated debate in the press, through such articles as "What Is to Be Done with Ballet" (1925) and "On Ballet Reform" (1928–29). These polemics on ballet reform led to major dancers and choreographers being asked to respond to a questionnaire about the possible paths of development for choreography. Quite a few mutually exclusive ideas were put forward; perceptions of the future varied. Emmanuil Beskin saw it in "physical culture," a point of view already mentioned. A more curious suggestion came from A. Alexandrovich. Musing on the notion that the principles of romantic and classical drama should not be imposed upon contemporary ballet, he proposed that to achieve modernity, ballet should give up attempts to depict it directly.[16] Unfortunately, no one paid any attention to him then, because the question he raised touched on the very nature of ballet. Time has shown that you can reflect contemporary reality without using a contemporary plot; the "eternal" is closer to the art of choreography than the specific moments.

This makes it all the more unexpected to read a response to the questionnaire given by the magazine *Zhizn' iskusstva* [Life of Art]: "A dance performance with a contemporary plot is possible, of course, but plot is not a basic condition for a modern production."[17] Three years separated this statement by Valentina Ivanova, a marvelous character dancer of the Leningrad stage, from Alexandrovich's article, but ballet had taken another path by then. The argument was preparing the way for the birth of a new direction in the art of ballet—one that was fully formulated in the 1930s and given the name "choreodrama."

The theoretical apologists of choreodrama were Alexei Gvozdev and Ivan Sollertinsky. Although they disagreed on a number of issues in choreographic aesthetics (for instance, their views on classical dance per se), they were united in a vision of the future of ballet. Here is Gvozdev on the ballet artist: "The new ballet needs first of all an actor, for without him there is no theater, no substantial, necessary, and useful theater art."[18] And here is Sollertinsky: "In order to become expressive, dance must turn into danced drama, and the dancer into a choreographic actor."[19] The critics were basically negative about classical dance, although Gvozdev was more restrained and less categorical than Sollertinsky: he recognized classical dance as an opportunity to get away from "oblique reality," but he denied its psychological depth and celebrated ballet's tendency toward acrobatics. Sollertinsky was harsher: "The primacy of acrobatics over classical dance is that acrobatics can be ... theatricalized within the system of modern theater while classical dance cannot."[20] He recommended retaining classical dance only as a way of training the body. Thus, on the one hand both Gvozdev and Sollertinsky called for plotted ballet drama, but on the other, they proposed replacing classical dance with acrobatic elements. But time prompted another view of the development of ballet theater. The 1930s resolved the contradictions in the arguments of Gvozdev and Sollertinsky.

Taking Noverre's idea of ballet drama and adding pantomime and dance, both classical and character, and teaching the ballerina and the male dancer to be actors above all, they created the genre of "choreodrama." New tasks were set for the dancers: not to dance and act, but to act while dancing, which was accomplished in the best productions of that genre — *The Fountain of Bakhchisarai* and *Romeo and Juliet*. But soon the goal of "playing a role" became primary on the ballet stage. Not everyone could manage it, and it did not always suit dancers brought up in the classical system. Ballet soloist Alexander Pushkin wanted to dance, which as it happens he could do much better than act. As a performer, he was in conflict with the tendencies of his time.

Yet the very first choreodrama was an

encouraging experience for him. In 1932, Boris Asafyev's ballet *The Flames of Paris* premiered, staged by the famous theater director Sergei Radlov and the choreographer Vasily Vainonen. Not long before the premiere, Radlov wrote: "In short—the basis for a ballet performance must be dance, dance that does not destroy but instead strengthens and crowns the image created by the actor. Not abstractly formal innovation, but imbued with dramatic content—that is the path that will be followed by the art of ballet, enriched by new, socially saturated themes."[21]

These words make it clear that the experienced director played as important a part in the production as did Vainonen, the choreographer. Even though the director insisted that the basis of a ballet performance must be dance, that was not the case with their creation. Dance, which "strengthens and crowns the image created by the actor," was not the main means of expression in *The Flames of Paris*; the ballet's action developed primarily in dramatic pantomime. Acting took preeminence, and only in the divertissement did dance triumphantly reclaim its primacy. In other words, *The Flames of Paris* failed to merge expressive acting with the dance fabric of the production. Its best fragments live to this day in many theaters (the famous pas de deux, the Basque dance), but the ballet as a whole has been relegated to history.

As the choreodrama became established, artists began to appear who stressed acting over dancing. After *The Flames of Paris* and *The Fountain of Bakhchisarai*, the names Ulanova, Vecheslova, Iordan, Anisimova, Sergeyev, Chabukiani, and Dudko took on a new excitement. In many ways, their work characterized the Soviet ballet of the period; it was they who raised the acting mastery of ballet dancers to unprecedented heights.

Keeping in mind that the 1930s were the formative period of the Soviet style of ballet, we must admit that the innovations brought into the ballet by theater directors were not always organic. Of course, the director taught the choreographer to operate in dance in a certain way, but at the same time he created barriers that had to be overcome by pantomime. Nevertheless, even *The Flames of Paris* was a popular success—the critics hailed the appearance of a heroic ballet that for the first time on the ballet stage depicted "The People" as fighters overthrowing their oppressors. In addition, the new, innovative approach toward dance, including classical dance, triumphed in the best scenes. An example is the pas de quatre of Jeanne, her brother, Pierre, and Jerome and Philippe from Marseilles.

In Act 1, scene 2, when the revolutionary unit from Marseilles, rushing to Paris to help the insurrectionists, liberates the old man, Gaspard, from the castle of the Marquis de Beauregard, the palace courtyard becomes the site of an expression of stormy joy by the people. And after the farandolle comes the pas de quatre, danced by Iordan, Chabukiani, Shavrov, and Pushkin. Gvozdev mentions the pas de quatre: "Overcoming the unusual difficulties for a dancer primarily devoted to dramatic acting during a technically difficult dance, this 'quartet' reflects the important progress of the young choreographer toward the necessary reworking of the traditions of classical dance."[22]

Thus, Pushkin's name is linked with "dramatic acting." And this, from a review by E. Gershuni: "Shavrov and Pushkin, together with the entire troupe of the men from Marseilles, found expressive images that were particularly successfully embodied in dance in the pas de quatre of Act 1."[23] The dance of the four men seemed to rise from the joyous agitation of the masses. It was initiated by Jerome—Vakhtang Chabukiani, whose dancing animated the dance picture planned by the choreographer, resembling live, passionate speech. But these new directions were born in the truly expressive alloy of classic and character dancing. Pushkin always distinguished himself when he could dance;

Alexander Pushkin as Vaclav in *The Fountain of Bakhchisarai*.

his blending of dance technique and acting abilities was not as organic as Chabukiani's or Shavrov's, but his professionalism allowed him to appear successfully beside these brilliant dancer-actors.

Ten years of stage performances went by. We might say that Pushkin the dancer reached his limits. All his finest qualities—sense of pose, purity of execution of classical steps, and a soft leap—had been formed, and there is no doubt that he knew how to work. It is not surprising that at least a few leading roles appeared in his repertoire.

It was 1935. Pushkin wrote in his diary: "On December 24, I performed for the first time the role of Asak with Mungalova [he is referring to Lopukhov's ballet *The Ice Maiden* with music by Edvard Grieg]. Of course, on the 22nd and 23rd I rehearsed at the theater with a fever of 38 C and at the performance on the 24th it was 37.5 C. I would go to the rehearsals straight from bed, rehearse, and back to bed to take all kinds of sweat-inducing medicines. However, I was firmly determined to dance on the 24th; after all, I had managed all the rehearsals." Pushkin was a man of willpower, a quality always appreciated in the theater. He did not have the natural qualities of a premier dancer in the heroic style (impressive looks, exciting turns, dynamic flight in his jumps), nor was he a lyrical dancer, even though he performed in *Chopiniana*. He was distinguished by a flawless mastery of classical dance, and a mastery of support in a duet. (He actually began his teaching career as a teacher of partnering.) In the part of Asak, partnering qualities were extremely important. Petr Gusev, the leading exponent of this role, was a brilliant partner, and his duet with Olga Mungalova is part of the history of Soviet ballet as an example of total mastery of poses and lifts in an acrobatic adagio.

While he could handle duets in the virtuoso manner, as confirmed by his work in *The Ice Maiden*, Pushkin was lost when it came to emotional acting, and ballet

Alexander Pushkin as the Youth in *Chopiniana*.

Alexander Pushkin as the Youth, and Nina Zheleznova as a Sylphide, in *Chopiniana*.

Top: Vladimir Fidler and Alexander Pushkin as Polish lords in *The Fountain of Bakhchisarai*.

Alexander Pushkin as the Troubadour, and Olga Mungalova as the Friend of Juliet, in *Romeo and Juliet*.

was moving more and more toward drama. There appeared in quick succession *The Fountain of Bakhchisarai* and *Lost Illusions* by Zakharov, a new version of Vaganova's *Esmeralda*, Leonid Lavrovsky's *Katerina*, Vasily Vainonen's *Partisan Days*, and so on. More and more frequently, the struggle for the realistic style, for the primacy of plot in dance, boiled down to a struggle with dance itself. Does that mean that Pushkin did not perform at all in the new ballets? Certainly not. In the latter half of the 1930s, he was perhaps busiest of all.

    1936. January 24—*The Ice Maiden*. Asak. "This was my first time dancing with Zheleznova," he wrote in his diary. "It went well. For me, this second performance was calmer, I knew it all, so I walked out onto the stage confidently."

    January 28—*Lost Illusions*. "I performed once as Lucien's friend."

    January 30—the premiere of *Katerina*. "I dance the part of Zefir with Zubkovsky in Act II. We dance the variation together. Katerina is danced by Iordan."

    The diary shows how intensively Pushkin worked on the new repertoire. In February of that year he prepared the roles of the Khan in *The Little Hump-backed Horse* and the Conductor in *Lost Illusions*.

    Pushkin was not endowed with good health, but he never gave in to his illnesses. A frequent notation in his diaries reads: "I've been feeling bad all the time, I've got a cold," and next to it is the name of the performance in which he danced. The list of his performances shows that he was dancing every three or four days in this period. For instance, in *Lost Illusions* every month brought a new role: January, the Friend; February, the Conductor; March, the Chef. What was happening? A search for his proper emploi? Or the ability to learn a role and replace another dancer on short notice? The latter is more likely. Xenia Yurgenson, Pushkin's wife, used to say, "He could always replace any performer."[24] Pushkin was a real professional, and it was his profound professionalism that became the foundation of his teaching career.

Later, Pushkin the teacher often told his students: "If you can't last the class, you won't be able to last the performance." This was his golden rule during his performing years as well. "Self-preparation, responsibility—these were the qualities that distinguished Pushkin always," continued Yurgenson. "As he prepared, he was always working toward the stage image."

This needs to be emphasized: "As he prepared, he was always working toward the stage image." It may be the main trait that characterizes Pushkin the dancer. Daily training was not only the foundation of creativity but also the very "edifice" of the art, whereas the "penthouse" was the stage variations. Pushkin was not remembered for interesting roles, but to this day, when the pas de trois from *Swan Lake* is being rehearsed in a ballet studio, you can hear, "Pisarev and Pushkin were the best at the sissonne ouverte with an effacée and extension." As Vaganova did in her day, Pushkin achieved purity and finish in every step, in every connecting movement. When, many years later, he showed his students a tombée pas de bourrée, the step, even when performed at half-strength, seemed like a light puff of air. With a soft gliding movement across the floor, without a single jump, he moved imperceptibly over a long distance. It is soloists like this, with perfect mastery of all the tricky steps of classical dance, and perhaps with a touch of pedantry, who as a rule make the best teachers.

It was no accident that only seven years after his graduation performance—in 1932, at the peak of his performing career—Pushkin returned to the choreographic school, this time as a teacher of classical and duet dancing. This early turn to teaching can be explained in various ways. First of all, the ballet was attracting wider audiences, which had been lost in the late 1920s. One of the methods of confirming and extending this success was to bring in well-trained young artists as teachers. Who could have recommended Pushkin? Certainly, his teacher Vladimir Ponomarev. Pushkin had often substituted for Ponomarev at his lessons, and quite successfully.

Another reason was his dissatisfaction with his work in the theater. He had the ability, there was a need—and so Pushkin began teaching. This helped in his stage work, too. He had to test his knowledge, create combinations, and think about training students. So the recent graduate and young artist became a beginning teacher. But teaching had not yet become the main aspect of his life.

Work in the theater was growing more difficult. Even though the ballets of the 1930s used classical dance, Pushkin felt no affinity for them, since his abilities did not fully suit the new demands. Thus his personal peaks remained the classical pas de deux and variations.

1927. January 24—*Giselle*.

1928. "I was occupied in *Giselle*. I danced with O. Berg in Act 1. It went well. I danced excellently. I was praised by Chabukiani, V. I. Ponomarev, Pisarev, and others."

Pushkin would not have heard praise about his work in the new ballets.

But the new in ballet was being forged in conflict. Some critics felt that ballet had taken the wrong path, and that there was no unity among the performers, either. A weighty response to the too-fervent adherents of "dramatic" acting on the ballet stage came from Chabukiani's works. His heroes lived in dance that did not require plot justification. "Joyous" was what critics called Chabukiani's first ballet, *The Heart of the Hills* (1938), and a year later came *Laurencia*, which brought success not only to the leading dancers. For the first time in the 1930s, critics talked about the dance responsibilities of the corps de ballet, the leading

Natalya Kamkova and Alexander Pushkin in the pas de deux from *Giselle*.

Alexander Pushkin and Nadezhda Bazarova in "Black and White" from *Bolt*.

dancers, and the soloists. And wherever there is talk about dance, we come across Pushkin's name. Lubov Blok wrote, "The interestingly constructed variation of the two men, in which Gofman does not appear very confident, is marvelously danced by Pushkin."[25]

Pushkin was usually lucky in "twos." The two youths in *The Fountain of Bakhchisarai*, two in *Laurencia*, later two in *Cinderella*. At the same time he occasionally danced lead roles: the Prince in *The Nutcracker*, Vaclav in *The Fountain of Bakhchisarai*. He danced with the ballerinas Elena Lukom, Nina Mlodzinskaya, Olga Mungalova, and Nina Zheleznova. In 1939, he danced with Alla Shelest the famous duet of Diana and Acteon in the ballet *Esmeralda*, and in *The Little Humpbacked Horse* the duet of the Genius of the Ocean and the Pearl with Vera Osokina. In his last premiere before the war, *Romeo and Juliet*, he danced the Troubadour, a small, purely dance role. These roles did not radically change either his manner of performance or his artistic career.

How could he compete with Chabukiani in the role of Acteon? In Acteon's passionate scene, Chabukiani embodied Acteon's passion in headlong jetés and driving tours chaînés that seemed to cut through the space of the stage. It was clear that next to such outstanding dancers as Chabukiani, Konstantin Sergeyev, Semyon Kaplan, and Nikolai Zubkovsky, Pushkin was merely an excellent soloist, and that he could not aspire to being a premier dancer. The very fact that he sometimes performed leading roles meant quite a bit.

Fifteen years of his stage career went by, but instead of bringing a gradual relaxation, this period was a time of trial, a test of spiritual and physical strength. It was wartime. Personal cares and concerns took a backseat—everyone gave to the common cause what he could. Pushkin gave his gift as a professional. In the war years, in the city of

Alexander Pushkin as the Merchant in the pas d'Esclave from *Le Corsaire*.

Alexander Pushkin as Acteon in the pas de deux from *Esmeralda*.

Perm, to which the theater had been evacuated, he had to dance almost all the leading roles. They were not really within his powers, but it was necessary. And so the roles of Siegfried, Frondoso, and Basil appeared in his repertoire.

You might call it an artistic triumph of sorts. Everyone had his own battle lines, his own hardships to overcome, and everyone worked to overcome them without stinting. This is made clear in the few lines of gratitude in Decree 51, "On the Molotov Oblast [Region] Department of the Arts, May 7, 1942," where among the names of leading masters of the theater is Alexander Pushkin. And we can find Pushkin's name as well among those of the teachers at the choreographic Institute during the war years. He did not forget his second profession; it had become an inextricable part of his life, perhaps even the most important one.

On May 29, 1944, the first echelon of performers left Perm for Leningrad, including a large contingent of artists from the Kirov Theater. The theater was going home. Had anything changed in Pushkin's situation uponhis return? Yes and no. There was more talk of Pushkin the teacher: "First we must mention the strict and demanding master pedagogues A. Ya. Vaganova, B. V. Shavrov, M. F. Romanova, S. V. Shiripina, and A. I. Pushkin,"[26] wrote Alexander Movshenson in an article about the graduation performance for 1947. Life was moving onto a new track. New interests and concerns emerged.

And what about the theater? Here, too, Pushkin remained faithful to himself. In 1945, the theater marked his twentieth anniversary on the stage with a commemorative address. And once again we see Pushkin's name among the participants in the pas de trois in yet another revival of *Swan Lake*. In the same year, Pushkin danced *Chopiniana* with the young Ninel Petrova. The critics responded in their usual way to his 1946 performance in *Cinderella* (Konstantin Sergeyev's first production): "The second youth

(Babanov) is very light in his dancing, but he is not always in harmony with his always impeccably prepared partner (Pushkin)."²⁷ And this after twenty-one years in the theater! After the difficult war years! Only a self-sacrificing approach to art allowed Pushkin to continue dancing with his habitual thoroughness and ardor. His old injuries were acting up, but he was not one to complain, even though it was getting harder for him to take up his station.

Students are lined up at the barres: beginners as well as honored artists. The class is being taught by the still performing soloist Alexander Pushkin. His speech unhurried, a slightly slower movement of the arms, but completely centered.

That's the way he was in 1939. That's the way he was in 1945. And that's how his students of 1970 remember him.

Today's ballet is dealing with problems different from those of the days of Pushkin the dancer. The most troubling question for ballet then—to be or not to be—is long forgotten. But as we celebrate our victories, we must not forget those who fought hard to bring them about, who spent years struggling against the prejudice and extremism of the new times. One remembers that while reading these words, written in 1940: "The rejection of male classical dance is inexplicable. It is all the more incomprehensible since, thanks to marvelous teachers with a rare knowledge of the subject, we have a great number of brilliant classical dancers of whom we can be sincerely proud: Chabukiani, Sergeyev, Kaplan, Ermolayev, Messerer, Komarov, Pushkin, Pisarev, and Fidler."²⁸

A few more years passed, and from among those brilliant dancers there arose a new generation of teachers. And probably the most outstanding of them all was Alexander Ivanovich Pushkin.

Alexander Pushkin as the Youth in *Laurencia*.

Legacy

CHAPTER 2

Pushkin always told his students: "Remember those who came before you." And unafraid of diminishing his personal authority, he demonstrated yet again his crystal-pure honesty at the evening celebrating the seventy-fifth birthday of his mentor, Vladimir Ivanovich Ponomarev. "We remember this marvelous teacher of men's dancing with warmth and sincerity…. He always shared his experience, his knowledge, with me, and I learned a great deal from him as a performer and as a teacher."[1]

The first meeting between Pushkin and Ponomarev took place in March 1923, when fifteen-year-old Sasha was accepted at the Academic Theater School. He went on studying with Ponomarev right up to his graduation, preparing his role in the graduation performance of *La Source* under Ponomarev's direct supervision. And later, as a soloist in the ballet, for many years Pushkin worked daily in Ponomarev's master class for theater artists. It was from Ponomarev that he acquired the traditions of the St. Petersburg school of dance and the traditions of St. Petersburg pedagogy. But Ponomarev, in turn, had based his work on the experience and knowledge of his own mentors and teachers and was the heir to the glorious traditions of many outstanding teachers. They were such luminaries as Christian Johansson, the Swedish-born comrade-in-arms of Petipa, and the Italian Enrico Cecchetti, and after them, as if growing out of those two mighty roots, came a long line of brilliant teachers—Ekaterina Vazem, Evgenia Sokolova, Pavel Gerdt, Olga Preobrazhenskaya, Nikolai Legat, Mikhail Obukhov—a line that extended directly through Preobrazhenskaya and Legat to Agrippina Vaganova and Vladimir Ponomarev, teachers of the Soviet era.

In 1895, Ivan Vsevolozhsky, director of the imperial theaters, convened a meeting of ballet teachers to clarify "why at the St. Petersburg Theater School the instruction in ballet dancing does not achieve the desired

Vladimir Ponomarev (1892–1951).

results."[2] The school's leading masters, Johansson and Pavel Gerdt, felt that despite the ascendancy of Cecchetti, whose method of teaching had attracted many dancers, it was short-sighted to ignore innovation. Petipa himself had come to that realization even earlier, and readily hired students of the Italian school for his ballets. He had entrusted the most difficult parts in *The Sleeping Beauty* to Italian dancers: Carlotta Brianza danced Aurora and Cecchetti the Blue Bird. In characterizing the situation of that period, Volynsky later wrote: "Merging with the French school, Italian technique, so vivid and animated, so responsive to the realities of the moment, had done good service in renewing ballet. It was a healthy reaction against the cult of beauty, entrenched in France and brought from there to Russia by foreign ballet masters."[3]

Changes began a year after the meeting. In 1896, Cecchetti, who had not been permitted to teach anything other than mime, an auxiliary subject, was appointed senior teacher of the women's department of the school. Pavel Gerdt became the senior teacher in the men's department. (The position itself was introduced at the same time.) But at first this innovation led only to a sharper differentiation between the two different systems of teaching.

The Italian master's class was strict and did not permit any improvisations. Cecchetti gave his students a reliable technique that had not been seen before, including dynamic turns, strength of toes, and power in the legs, especially in lifts. Quick turns were achieved by a sharp "force" (reserve of power), in which the legs pushed off from the floor while simultaneously the arms moved from the preparatory position to the one needed for turns. In Cecchetti's method, the head played a very important part in the turn, directing the movement.

In Cecchetti's class, much attention was also paid to the approaches, the linking steps. They took on three-dimensionality, an inner energy that then found release in the jumps. The dynamism of all dance movements began with the exercises at the barre. One could reject the rather harsh manner of executing certain steps that was characteristic of the Italian school, but its approach to training had real advantages. In the final analysis, Cecchetti's school inculcated permanent skills in dynamic turns and jumps, cleanly etched stops, and precise tempo. The movements of the arms, body, and legs took on confidence and expression.

To develop agility and ease in turning and sharpness and elasticity in jumps, Cecchetti applied his new approach to footwork. He offered ten movements of the foot in which he tried to capture all its possible positions during dancing. And his requirement—"Do not let them [the insteps] relax either in strength or elasticity"[4]—is very timely today, when classical dance has been enriched by free movement in which footwork is given a very important place.

Tending toward the pedantic, Cecchetti tried to establish a precise system for everything. He implemented a strict structure for his class. For every day of the week there was a definite lesson plan, a highly regimented "menu" of sequences that included a large number of movements from classical dance. This cycle was repeated week after week. The structure of the daily class was directed toward the systematic mastery of certain movements, which gave them polish and flawlessness. Such a class can sometimes be exhausting, and sometimes, when the barrier is quickly overcome, it may seem inadequate, since it keeps the dancer trapped in a circle of prescribed choreographic vocabulary. This was a class with only one goal, one idea.

In this regard, the tradition of the St. Petersburg school was different. Johansson's memoirs constantly mention that he never repeated a sequence of movements; therefore, if a particular combination of steps didn't work for a dancer, he couldn't be sure that he'd have an opportunity to repeat it. On the other hand, we must not

Christian Johansson (1817–1903). Enrico Cecchetti (1850–1928).

Pavel Gerdt (1844–1917).   Mikhail Fokine (1880–1942).

forget that a master like Johansson developed technique in every lesson with each new sequence of dance steps. This kind of training demands a subtle pedagogical sense, the ability to create a sequence whose very construction is educational. Later, this principle would become the linchpin of Russian ballet teaching, especially as practiced by Pushkin.

The methodology of mastering virtuoso dance that predominated in Cecchetti's classes did not easily gain acceptance in St. Petersburg. The apologists for academic norms resisted stubbornly, and Johansson's followers were much less tolerant than the patriarch himself. This applies to Pavel Gerdt, the leading teacher in the men's department (he periodically gave women's classes, too), who was also the brilliant premier dancer of the Maryinsky stage.

Having devoted almost a quarter of a century (from 1880) to pedagogy, Pavel Andreyevich Gerdt remained a star and artist first. He did not create a unique pedagogical system, but his memory and his wonderfully trained body fixed the history of ballet during the Petipa era. His demonstrations invariably had perfection of line, purity of position, and flawlessness in the French style—everything for which Petipa's theater was famed, based as it was on the Johansson school. Gerdt's personality had a magical effect on his students. They forget that the first part of class (exercise at the barre and in the center of the room) was traditional and did not differ from the assignments of most other teachers. Toward the end of class, the most important part began: the teacher demonstrated fragments of dances from ballets no longer in the repertoire. Tamara Karsavina recalled how reluctantly she left class, even though she was exhausted, "looking forward to to-morrow, when perhaps 'the dance with a shadow,' the Masterpiece of Cerrito, would be gone through again."[5] But one had to be able to understand what Gerdt demonstrated, because he did not bother with preparation and details and sometimes not even with elementary exercises.

According to Mikhail Fokine, "He was not a teacher by nature, and did not insist on anything. You had to know how to learn from him in order to extract all the benefit from that embodiment of gracefulness."[6]

Naturally, Cecchetti's pedagogy was alien in every way to Gerdt. Nikolai Legat paid more attention to it, albeit critically.

By 1904, when Gerdt stopped teaching to devote himself to performing (and the year before Cecchetti moved abroad and Johansson died in Stockholm), Legat, who had been teaching at the theater school since 1896, had become the senior authority among the teachers of St. Petersburg. At his side were the young Mikhail Fokine and Mikhail Obukhov.

Legat's mature work belongs to another era, when the old contradictions had softened noticeably, making way for new conflicts. In the first decade of the twentieth century, all art forms took on a particularly tense and stormy character. Along with the rest of the intelligentsia, writers, performers, and artists were looking into the future with growing anxiety, tormented by the "damned questions" of the times. This was the source of neo-romantic themes in art, some turning to an idealized past, others to heroic characters and images. Like no other art form, the ballet united artists of varying persuasions. The poetics of the Symbolists manifested themselves in the works of Petersburger Fokine, who found like-minded thinkers in the *Mir iskusstva* [World of Art] group. In Moscow, Alexander Gorsky was finding inspiration in the characters of Hugo and Flaubert.

The year 1907—the year Pushkin was born—was marked by two events that brought about enormous shifts in the development of choreography. That was the year that the Maryinsky Theater, the citadel of ballet academism, permitted within its walls Fokine's first major choreographic production, *Le Pavillon d'Armide*, based on the libretto and designs of Alexandre Benois to the music of Nikolai Tcherepnin (before this production, Fokine had been limited to graduation performances at the school and to benefit evenings). And at the same time, a former official of the imperial theater management, Sergei Diaghilev, successfully launched concerts of Russian symphonic music in Paris, which allowed him a year later to produce there a brilliant season of Russian opera starring Fyodor Chaliapin, and beginning the year after that to hold regular Russian Seasons abroad, concentrating on ballet.

The new was knocking at the doors of the "official" imperial theater. It could be ignored, rejected, and even fought, but no one could stop these new sprouts on the tree of academic art. Of course, even Fokine's productions when accepted into the theater's repertoire (*Le Pavillon d'Armide* was followed in quick succession by *Eunice* and *Chopiniana*) did not shake the foundations of the imperial ballet. In 1909, with the first ballet season in Paris, the argument between the "academics" and the "reformers" moved beyond Russia's borders. The old and the new no longer clashed on only one stage. Fokine's epochal works after *Chopiniana*—*Polovtsian Dances*, *Schéhérazade*, *Firebird*, *Petrouchka*, and many others—formed the repertoire of the Russian Seasons.

The contentious situation in Russian ballet had an impact on the school. It was impossible to preserve peace in the sanctum sanctorum, the theater school.

On March 29, 1909, Legat, the leading specialist in classical dance of the St. Petersburg school, did not appear with the other teachers at the examinations of Fokine's ballerinas. This was the beginning of the crisis in the pedagogical process of the school, which became the arena of stormy clashes between the academic Legat and the iconoclast Fokine. In Moscow, hostility divided the dancer and teacher Vasily Tikhomirov and the ballet master Alexander Gorsky. The conflict had developed gradually. When the talented young dancer Fokine was asked in 1901 to teach the younger pupils, he was pleased at the prospect of doing something new in the class. And although many years later he recalled, "I think that at the time I was trying to hold back from any new experiments and just be the guardian of traditions and rules developed over the centuries,"[7] that was not quite the case. Of course, in 1901 Fokine, although dissatisfied by the situation in ballet, did not have a program of change, and of course, as a neophyte teacher, he zealously taught his students everything that he had learned from his mentor, Nikolai Legat. And even in 1906, the preparation of Fokine's graduates was perfectly fine with Legat himself— they included, in particular, Elena Smirnova, who had a flawless command of classical dance. But in his dreams Fokine saw poses emancipated from the canonic positions, an épaulement that had its own aesthetic value, and a port de bras that artistically framed the classic steps. Meeting the people of *Mir iskusstva* not only turned everything he had learned in childhood upside down, it also showed him the way to satisfy his own strivings. Class became the first place where he could realize his creative ideas. Understanding the need for physical work to develop agility and strength, Fokine nevertheless worried that "these gymnastics can kill the feel for dance."[8] But for Legat "these gymnastics" were the art itself. Consequently, he gave the best dancers of Fokine's graduating class of 1909, Elena Lukom and Lidia Lopuhova, a grade of 6 ("not completely satisfactory") out of 12.

Of course, Legat was irritated by students who during a classical dance lesson tried to run and walk rhythmically, seeking movements that corresponded to serious ("not ballet") music. Lukom recalled, "We were asked to improvise a dance to brief excerpts of musical works and to create our own dance variations."[9] In his dream of new expressive means, Fokine seemed to have forgotten the school's primary demand—maintaining a literate execution of all the movements of the ballet catechism—as he tried to develop the creative imagination of his students. He considered the academic canon the heaviest chain encumbering contemporary ballet. And he tried a few things in his class, attempting to expand the borders of the port de bras, to find a fresh approach to exercise sequences in the center of the room. Of course, choreography for Diaghilev was taking up more of Fokine's time, frequently distracting him from the school. In 1911, he left the school for good.

As a result, the work of Fokine's antagonist, Legat, became the decisive factor in the future of ballet pedagogy. Legat is a controversial figure. Educated by Gerdt, he graduated in 1888 from the school, where he met the idols of Russian ballet academism: Marius Petipa and Christian Johansson. The young dancer had whole-heartedly accepted the aesthetic precepts of the great choreographer. In class, Johansson revealed to him the limitless "reserves" of classical dance, frequently amazing the thoughtful young artist with the originality of his class assignments.

However, Cecchetti had a strong influence on the dancer, too. The technique of the Italians "was distinguished by remarkable dexterity and sensational brilliance,"[10] Legat recalled in his mature years in his 1932 book *The Story of the Russian School*, describing how he had learned from them how to control his body as well as new methods for doing turns. The young artist devoted considerable attention to technical perfection, but he did not copy other virtuosi. "I was anxious to acquire the Italian technique," he wrote, "and adapt it to our school."[11] Legat did not recognize technique as the goal of choreography, even though he was sometimes criticized for his coolness as a dancer. In fact, he was at his best in the role of a simpleton lover. He was incomparable as Colin (*La Fille Mal Gardée*) and Franz (*Coppélia*), but his acting abilities were not suited to playing princes. Here he lost out to the impressive Gerdt; his regal bearing seemed borrowed. There was an analogous situation later in the failure of his work as ballet master, in his attempt to reanimate the fairy spectacle ballets of the days of Petipa.

Fokine was justified in saying about him: "N. G. Legat was a very gifted man. [But] one trait hindered him both in his career as a dancer and in his work as a ballet master and teacher. He gave much to Russian ballet, but he could have given much more. He was a slave to tradition.... The times were changing. Everything was changing in every form of art ... but Legat's ideals were unchanged."[12]

We can accept Fokine's estimate of Legat the dancer and ballet master, but his opinion of Legat the teacher is quite unfair. Undoubtedly, Legat did not change his views on the instruction of classical dance, as did Fokine himself. Rather, he passed on what he had learned in the classes taught by his father, the dancer and teacher Gustav Legat, by Pavel Gerdt, and by Johansson. But although remaining a confirmed academist, he was a talented and creative teacher. Johansson's care and support are noteworthy; he encouraged Legat's desire to teach, and in 1904, Legat replaced Johansson as teacher of the class for the theater's soloists, who included Mathilde Kchessinska, Vera Trefilova, Anna Pavlova, Lydia Kyasht, Tamara Karsavina, Agrippina Vaganova, Mikhail Fokine, and Adolf Bolm. And he accurately noted in his book that his assignment to this position was well received by the company.

Legat's pedagogy was based on the vitality of classical dance in the Russian school, and in this he was more farsighted than Fokine. As Lopukhov put it, "If Legat had kept records of his lessons, if he could have told us why he demanded one thing from this student and another from that one, we would have a priceless aid today for teaching classical dance and raising talented ballet artists."[13] Unfortunately, Legat did not leave such a work. The book about the Russian school of ballet published in London gives only a superficial picture of his methods. The notes taken by his students—and they later worked all over the world—were lost in the bustle of artistic life. And still Legat's fundamental precepts are clear from his memoirs, the observations of his students, and the notes of ballet historians.

The basis of Legat's teaching was his subtle selection from the methods of Russian, French, and Italian masters. Lopukhov, who had studied in Legat's class, maintained, "Legat did not simply pass along to students what he had received from his own teachers. He worked long and hard to bring into a unified system the national and unique elements of classical dance that had been known long before. Therefore his students did not belong at all to the French school (as balletomanes insisted). They were vivid representatives of a new school of dance—truly Russian—which subsequently conquered the world."[14] It was Legat who first proclaimed the creation of a new school that defined the achievements of ballet artists of the twentieth century. His work was an important link in the chain of predecessors of today's Russian school of classical dance.

Trying to define Legat's methods, Lopukhov said, "Legat's pedagogy was, if I can put it that way, intelligent."[15] What predominated was not the elemental talent of a "creator" of ballet artists, but the labor of a teacher digesting the experiences accumulated by colleagues, teachers, and himself as a dancer.

Work in the theater had taught Legat that the atmosphere in class influences the receptivity of the students, which is why he tried "to lighten the burden of strenuous exercises by timely jokes and lively music."[16] He had a natural humor and a witty manner of parodying a failed sequence (Legat was a master of parody and had a talent for drawing, like his brother, Sergei Legat, a leading dancer of the Maryinsky Theater). He valued the joy his students felt when they mastered a difficult assignment.

Legat prepared his lessons ahead of time. He enjoyed demonstrating, and did it well, taking pleasure in displaying the beauty of classic steps. None of his class assignments grew out of improvisation. "The class was created according to a definite plan from beginning to end," writes Lubov Blok, a historian of classical dance. "Everything done at the barre was a preparation for what would be done in the adagio, and the allegro was the resolution of the tension."[17] And according to Blok, "Legat changed his lesson daily in relation to the current assignment."[18] This allows me to conclude that Legat had a definite concept for his class. Cecchetti had first introduced this methodological principle. Vasily Tikhomirov, the Moscow master, developed it in his own way. But Legat was of course more flexible than Cecchetti in the selection of movements and sequences in his daily exercises. The "current assignment" and the idea of the lesson were determined by his concern for the individual students and artists in his class. The technical level demanded of each student was in accordance with his specific abilities at that particular stage of his training. This was the "intelligence" of Legat's method.

Legat realized that without a mastery of the alphabet of an art, art is impossible; therefore, he sought to develop the technique of dance through his methods of instruction. Diligently and lovingly polishing the details of execution of each step, he did not worry about emotional and stylistic aspects. The manner of execution and the aesthetic precepts willed to him by the nineteenth century remained inviolable to him. That is the fundamental difference between him and Fokine, whose pedagogic interests were closely tied to a creative seeking for modernity, and who insisted upon an aesthetic essence in the execution of steps. Fokine felt oppressed by the "dead" paradigms of mandatory classical exercises. Legat, on the other hand, could spend hours seeking through various combinations of connecting steps to find the most rational preparation for executing a turn or jump. Rationality in ways of executing steps and in methods of instruction would later be the hallmark of the methodology of Agrippina Vaganova and her followers.

The development and greater complexity of the technique of dance brought with it the necessity for the fastest possible warm-up of muscles in the first exercises at the barre, so that more time and attention could be devoted to the exercises—the adagio and jumps—in the center of the room. So Legat changed the usual order of movements in the exercises. "Since time immemorial, for instance, work began with a plié in five positions. But Legat," wrote Lopukhov, "started his class with battement tendu."[19] Personal experience had shown the teacher that the heavy plié did not help prepare muscles for what was to follow, so he placed the battement tendu in first place in the exercise at the barre. All the muscles of the legs are involved in a battement tendu, and the load is spread evenly, without causing overstrain, which is important at the start of work. Today, many teachers follow that shift in order.

Moreover, concerned to provide the fastest possible preparation of the muscles before work began on the complex adagio and virtuoso allegro, Legat let his students use exercise equipment and massage (the ligaments are stretched by external force, active massage). Later, Vaganova would be categorically opposed to the introduction of such auxiliary methods into the classical dance class, but this matter is still in dispute today. The expansion of the borders of classical dance and the increased difficulty of technique demands greater resilience from the dancer's body; sometimes the auxiliary methods are necessary. Legat thought long and hard about how to develop the physical abilities of his students, and his ideas led him beyond the framework of classical exercises. His experience helped teachers of subsequent generations remove their blinkers and turn to elements of gymnastics and a knowledge of the sports world.

The class continued. "In the center, please!" And the students took their places in the center of the rehearsal hall. Legat wrote that he changed the combination of movements on the floor every day.[20] Only the main forms of temps lié were invariably repeated. This exercise is a chain of gentle développé and dégagé, framed by a port de bras. It develops stability, coordination, and fluidity of transition from one pose to another—the most basic qualities for mastering classical dance.

The teacher played a simple improvisation on the piano. The students followed the line of the melody. Legat watched for purity of leg positions, fluidity in the demi-plié, the precise direction of the head. If he needed to call attention to an error, his fingers froze on the keyboard. After a quick explanation of the mistake, he took up the interrupted melody.

The conclusion of the class was the allegro. "Legat did not have any special methods for learning turns, jumps, or beats," Blok notes. "He gradually led up to them. He would assign a combination that made turns an inevitability. He would prepare a jump so that there would be elevation and power. He knew the very roots of a movement."[21] To gradually bring a student to the proper execution of a complex step is a marvelous quality in a teacher. This perspicacious teacher made his assignments incredibly comfortable. His students mastered the material easily, often not even realizing that every lesson involved an increase in technical complexity. Combinations followed one after another, often culminating in tours en l'air. Legat liked a neatly fixed fifth position at the end of an air turn, and he demanded a deep demi-plié upon landing, never tiring of repeating that this protects the knees and back from injury. Legat always protected his students from dangerous muscular strain. For this reason, he excluded the grand plié in fourth position, because it often damages the knees.

His concern for his students did not keep Legat from assigning difficult lessons, however. Not every dancer could execute them fully. In his book, Legat describes an incident that took place when he first came to Paris. In 1908, a French dancer came to a class with Mathilde Kchessinska and asked permission to join the Russians. "In twenty minutes of my ordinary exercises," Legat wrote, "he was exhausted, excused himself on the ground of not feeling well, and that was the end of his lessons!"[22] The touring artists had two more parts of the class to get through before running through the most important parts of their program.

Legat's allegro gave a misleading impression. All the combinations were built quite simply. It might seem that in terms of what it covered, his allegro did not come up to the other parts of the class, but the complexity lay in the requirement that all turns and jumps be done "in both directions." That is, the sequence of movements was executed first on one leg, usually the right, and then on the left. Not everyone could comply. Vaslav Nijinsky, Fokine, Bolm, and Leontiev were the best performers of Legat's allegro; they weren't frightened of the turns repeated on both sides or the jumps that called for pushing off first with the right and then with the left foot.

The thoroughness of Legat's class work affected the students' dancing: it formed precision in positions, severity of pose, and clarity in the connecting steps. Legat wrote that "the very highest compliment he [Christian Johansson] ever paid anyone was: 'Now you may do that in public.'"[23] Legat could have said the same thing. This was how the St. Petersburg academic style was forged—from the classroom to the stage is only a step, and Legat's best students took that step boldly. Things were harder for their teacher. What was wise and true in class seemed dry and pedantic on the stage, particularly in his work as ballet master, which is why the

Nikolai Legat (1869–1937).

teacher and his famous students parted ways so quickly. Fokine argued with him constantly in classroom and onstage; Nijinsky bewildered him with his interpretation of Albrecht in *Giselle*; Leontiev, immediately after the revolution, waged an open argument with him on the future of the academic school of dance. New conditions dictated new views in art. Legat remained categorical in his convictions.

Neither a trip to Moscow nor temporary work at the Petrograd School of Russian Ballet brought him satisfaction. In 1922, Legat left his homeland forever. Years of continual travel began. Companies, cities, and countries shifted in a kaleidoscope. The English ballet, closest to him in spirit, became the final refuge for the former dancer, ballet master, and teacher of the Imperial stage, and the school Legat founded exists in London to this day; many celebrities of the Western ballet world have studied there. But his most important heirs remained on the street whose architecture formed the taste of student, dancer, and teacher. "Legat's school is an important unifying link between the Johansson era and Vaganova's,"[24] is how Vera Krasovskaya summed up the legacy of Legat the teacher.

Pushkin came into contact with Legat's methodology in Volynsky's ballet citadel when he took the class given by Legat's wife, the outstanding dancer Natalya Nikolayeva. Legat, who was in charge of choreographic education at the new studio, condescended to give the young man his attention. A precious memento for Pushkin was a photo (reproduced on page 69) that Legat gave him in the summer of 1922 (two months before his departure), with a joking inscription: "You, my boy, are Pushkin, while I'm only Legat." (Alexander Pushkin [1799—1837] was Russia's greatest poet.)

The connecting thread tied the Legat school to Pushkin in a different way, too: through his teacher Vladimir Ponomarev, who had studied with one of Legat's

Mikhail Obukhov (1879–1914).

and Cecchetti's greatest students—Mikhail Obukhov. He was one of the famous four who graduated in 1898—Lubov Egorova, Yulia Sedova, Mikhail Fokine, and Obukhov—and was celebrated as a virtuoso performer of classical variations. Just two years after graduation (very rare in ballet), he was hired as senior instructor for the boys' classes. In 1904, when Legat began giving the class in perfection at the Maryinsky Theater, Obukhov was asked to take over his students, a sign of great trust. With his exceptional mastery of the precepts of his mentors, Cecchetti and Legat, having tested what he had learned from them on the stage and compared it with the experience of his foreign colleagues (Obukhov traveled to France several times to learn from the Opéra School, the cradle of ballet academism), the young teacher instilled excellent technique and flawless professionalism in his charges. The class of 1908 was a triumph for Obukhov: he gave to the ballet stage Vaslav Nijinsky and Georgy Rozai. Later graduates included Boris Romanov (1909) and Victor Semenov (1912). A comrade-in-arms of Legat, Obukhov was wary of Fokine's attempts at choreography, concerned about the fate of his gifted charges whom he preferred to see in the classics. (Nevertheless, they found themselves as true artists in the Diaghilev company.) This lack of understanding did not preclude cooperation in teaching. Obukhov helped Petr Vladimirov, a student of Fokine's, graduate (1911), when the ballet master asked Obukhov to cover for him while he was abroad, working with Diaghilev. On the other hand, in 1910, when Obukhov took a leave abroad, Fokine brought his students to graduation, albeit not spending much time with them. Pushkin's teacher, Ponomarev, was in this class.

Vladimir Ivanovich Ponomarev and Agrippina Yakovlevna Vaganova open a new chapter in the history of Russian ballet pedagogy. The professional mastery of the traditionalist teachers Legat and Obukhov came to be less appreciated because of their old-fashioned aesthetic precepts and the gap between them and the innovative spirit of the times and avant-garde choreographic thought. Their work laid a solid foundation for the further development of dance technique, but it did include some qualities of stagnation that would be overcome by the next generation. Vaganova and Ponomarev focused on the future of ballet theater. Vaganova gave to the modern stage ballerinas who were not only marvelous but were also imbued with new dance qualities. And "out from under the wing" of Ponomarev, as the well-known dancer and pantomime actor Mikhail Mikhailov put it, "came all the artists of the Leningrad ballet who created a revolution in men's classical dance."[25] His students included Petr Gusev and Alexei Ermolayev, Vakhtang Chabukiani and Konstantin Sergeyev, Nikolai Zubkovsky and Semyon Kaplan, as well as the future ballet teachers Alexei Pisarev and Alexander Pushkin.

Ponomarev's teaching career, like Obukhov's, began very early. From 1913 he taught at the St. Petersburg (later, the Petrograd, and later still the Leningrad) Ballet School, and then led a class of soloists of the Kirov Theater of Opera and Ballet—in other words, he taught for almost four decades, until the end of his life. He was a ballet professional in the broadest sense of the word. Fyodor Lopukhov, who as director of the theater's ballet troupe in 1922–30 was very familiar with Ponomarev's performing career, wrote: "Ponomarev in the early years after the October Revolution could take the place of any classical dancer if necessary and always guarantee the proper level of performance."[26] His strict and graceful manner of dance, coupled with a total mastery of technique, allowed him in those years to dance Albrecht and Siegfried, even though he did not have a romantic appearance, as well as Franz, Colin, Harlequin, and many other roles. In those same years Ponomarev revived ballets of the classical repertoire for the choreographic school: *Talisman, Harlequinade, La Fille Mal*

Gardée. And in 1929 he created the dances for Act II in the Leningrad production of *The Red Poppy* and later performed in revivals of *La Bayadère, Giselle*, and other legacy ballets. Finally, in the mid-1930s, Ponomarev was assistant art director of the Kirov Ballet, in 1938–39 he headed the Maly Opera Theater, and during the war he was acting director of the Kirov Ballet in Perm. But his most important work was always teaching in the school and the soloists' class. Tirelessly, he formed a new generation of dancers.

Calm, balanced, Ponomarev created an atmosphere of seriousness and significance in his classes. According to his wife, he didn't make notations before class but prepared alone for a while and then entered the class, ready to work.[27] His combinations were simple and easy to remember. They developed coordination, strength, and agility. Asaf Messerer, who attended his class of perfection at the Kirov Theater, recounted, "Ponomarev's combinations were logical, one movement flowing out of the other. Besides that, he was strict about accuracy of execution of the canon, even though he made criticisms gently and as if in passing. You could tell that this was a kind and pleasant man…. Later, in Moscow I practiced the combinations that I had learned from Vladimir Ivanovich, which had a good effect on my technique."[28]

Everyone who talked about his mastery as a teacher inevitably added that he was a "kind, pleasant man." And in fact, Ponomarev explained his assignments in an even, restrained manner and made his corrections and remarks without any heat, which was quite rare in ballet rehearsal rooms. The atmosphere was quite different in Vaganova's classroom, according to many reminiscences. The tone of her comments could sometimes push a student to do the impossible, but it could also literally paralyze her. There was nothing like this in Ponomarev's class. His students were afraid of something else. "I'm not afraid that I will dance badly, but I do not want to let down Vladimir Ivanovich,"

Agrippina Vaganova (1879–1951).

Pushkin wrote in his diary on February 25, 1924, on the eve of the school's concert at the Alexandrinsky Theater. The program included Pugni's *Ondine, ou La Naiade*, staged by Ponomarev and Alexander Shiryaev for the students, and a concert division in which Pushkin danced a variation created for him by Ponomarev.

Of course, not all of Ponomarev's students obeyed him so loyally. Alexei Ermolayev, a 1925 graduate, flew over the stage in unprecedented jumps that tore through space, refuting the laws of academic ballet. Ermolayev was Ponomarev's pride, but perhaps also his secret heartache. His dancing was called "stormy" and "fierce." In a collection of tributes to Ermolayev, Petr Gusev recalls that when the young dancer was accepted into the theater, there was a group of starting dancers there who trained independently as well as in the general men's class. Trying to expand the boundaries of their art, they worked on technique. "Ermolayev," writes Gusev, "joined this group and probably hurt the feelings of his school instructor V. I. Ponomarev, in whose class everything was very sensible, academically severe, and calm. Too calm for those stormy times in art."[29] It would have been more accurate to say "Seemed too calm."

Ponomarev's academism cannot be overestimated—especially in "those stormy times." He was the reliable support for any technique, any virtuosity. Years later Ermolayev realized it. "I was taught," he admitted, "by good teachers. I am infinitely grateful to them to this day. And this obliges me to think about my students now, about what and how I must teach them."[30]

Pushkin always remained loyal to his teacher's principles and became his successor at the school and at the theater.

Pushkin and Ermolayev, two students of Ponomarev. The former believed fully in the inviolability of the precepts of the classical school, never doubting them.

The latter spent his life rejecting the conventional, in a hurry to take a step forward. Ponomarev's class prepared both for their creative lives.

A subtle understanding of the laws and norms of ballet academism manifested itself equally in Ponomarev's work as a teacher and ballet master. He appreciated the old classical variations, pas de deux, and pas de trois. Pushkin noted in his diary the variation from *The Naiad and the Fisherman* that he danced at the Alexandrinsky Theater and Colin's variations from *La Fille Mal Gardée*, revived by Ponomarev. Pushkin's notations on the variations and individual classes and the speech he made at the festivities for Ponomarev's seventy-fifth birthday give us a glimpse into this outstanding teacher's work. Strangely enough, there is very little left to show how he worked, and in this sense Pushkin's notes are unique.

There is only one sentence in Pushkin's diary about the first part of class, the exercises at the barre: "Every day there is an enormous exercise." Here Ponomarev continued in the tradition of Johansson's school, which demanded variety and complexity in the exercises. Varying the movements at the barre daily, he retained the unchanging structure (the order in which the combinations come), which goes back to Johansson. Vaganova maintained the same principle of structure for her class. Later, Pushkin did the same. Every day the students were offered new combinations of movements that developed strength, coordination, and lightness. The goal was to emancipate and at the same time to strengthen the dancer's body.

A 1924 notation about two adagios, planned by Ponomarev for the exams of the junior class, of which Pushkin was a member, gives an idea of the character of the work in the center of the room.

Ponomarev borrowed Vaganova's rational structure for the second part of his class, where for the sake of saving time, only three adagios that encompassed all the necessary movements were given, instead of all the exercises. Vaganova seemed to be doing away with exercises in the center of the room, but in fact she included them in these three adagio combinations. Pushkin recorded only two adagios. Apparently, it was only a year later that Ponomarev adopted the principle fully, because in 1925 Pushkin had notations for three adagios.

Vaganova recommended that the first, "small" adagio include plié with various battements développés and battements tendus. The battements tendus combination was present in Ponomarev's adagio, too. Later, in recording Pushkin's classes, his students usually did not detail the entire combination of battements tendus and battements tendus jetés, noting instead: "Then came the combination of battements tendus with jetés and pirouettes." The battements tendus combinations that crowned Ponomarev's adagio lessons are lost. Pushkin's corresponding combinations grow harder and harder to recall.

Here is an incomplete record of the adagio in the diary of seventeen-year-old Pushkin: "Grand plié in fifth position, right leg in front. Raise onto half-toe and pose [apparently, legs in fifth position and arms in third]. Battement développé with right leg croisée at 90 degrees (left arm in second, right in third), bring leg into pose à la seconde and carry through to pose fourth arabesque. Go back to the right leg, close the left leg in fifth position in front. Take it out into pose à la seconde, fouetté in position first arabesque, demi-plié and one circle in that pose. Slowly. Stop in pose attitude croisée, demi-plié and relevé in pose first arabesque. Lower left leg into fifth position forward. Repeat everything with the other leg."

Ponomarev built this complex combination carefully. Students who had completed the difficult transition of the right leg from croisée in front to the pose of fourth arabesque had to continue the movement in the second part of the adagio with the left leg, while the right became the supporting leg. This way the teacher achieved an equal test for both legs in this exercise. The adagio grows in complexity from the first movement to the last. The movement of the right leg from one pose to another is not easy, but in the second part of the adagio there is a fouetté from the à la seconde pose into the first arabesque—a movement that is much more complex. There was also a tour en dedans from first arabesque to an attitude croisée pose in the second part. Even within the combination, Ponomarev observed his main rule: from simple to complex.

Vaganova and Ponomarev divided the rehearsal studio into eight points.

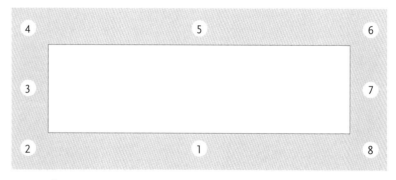

1–audience

The second adagio is the next step in raising technique to a greater complexity. There are transitions from pose to pose using the fouetté en tournant. For instance, the left leg in a croisée pose forward to point 2 (left arm in second, right in third position), fouetté en dedans to pose in fourth arabesque to point 8. This transition demands stable hip position in the working left leg and an open position of the supporting right leg and a coordinated turn of the body from one position to the other. The technique for turning in the second adagio is more complex than in the first. Here we encounter two tours en dedans in the à la seconde pose. This adagio begins with tours en dedans sur le cou-de-pied and ends with two tours en dehors in the à la seconde pose.

An analysis of both adagios shows that in this part of the class Ponomarev was paying greater attention to various forms of turning—turns are, of course, a very important aspect of classical dance. Ponomarev's students came to have an easy mastery of technically difficult pirouettes and various tours en l'air. Yuri Slonimsky wrote with delight about Ermolayev's turns: "Five or six pirouettes, the usual practice, he brought to ten to twelve and started changing poses while turning, which created an exceptional impression."[31] Ermolayev developed his virtuosity in turns through his fanatical diligence, but the fundamentals of turning, the "axis," the shape of arms and legs, came from Ponomarev. Slonimsky noted that Ermolayev "made a big pirouette, traveling along the diagonal across the stage, sometimes slowing the tempo, sometimes speeding it up."[32] That could only have been achieved through the skill in changing poses during a turn which he had mastered in class.

Ponomarev's classes laid the basis for the development of technical elements that expressed the aesthetic strivings of dancers of a new, more personal type. It was this masculine and personal style of dance that typified the new era in the work of his students, given the variety of their individual temperaments, tendencies, and artistic emploi. At the same time, his adagios taught them to execute their movements precisely or, as professionals say, "cleanly." The intense pursuit of virtuoso technique on the ballet stage in the 1920s did not muddy the wellspring of traditional schooling. The progressives imbued the contents of dance with new nuances that did not contradict its classical essence.

As important as exercises at the barre and the adagio are in dance training, the main part of the men's class is the allegro; it is in the allegro that all the acquired skills accumulate and the student masters the combinations that lead to dancing on the stage.

Of Ponomarev's general requirements for jump steps, the most notable was his heightened attention to a noiseless soft landing. The third phase of a jump (the first is the push off, the second, position in the air, and the third, the landing) is probably the most difficult and important. It is possible to push off easily, without apparent effort yet energetically, and to execute a complex revolution in the air, but to be unable to hold the necessary pose upon landing or to make so much noise that it ruins the impression of the jump. The highest, most dynamic jump has aesthetic value only when the position in the air clearly changes to the needed pose upon landing, and a springy, soft plié extends the pose. Ponomarev tirelessly inculcated this ability in his students. Another special concern of his was the plié before the push off. It is no wonder that the critics of those years wrote about the "flying" abilities of the Leningrad dancers, who seemed to fly off effortlessly, unlike the Muscovites, who achieved height with a sharp push. Landing in a deep demi-plié, Ponomarev's students created the illusion of a lengthy flight. To increase the effect of lightness and softness, the dancers of the Ponomarev school used the pas chassé in the connecting moves, more of a glide than the dynamic steps used by the Moscow school.

The pas glissade, pas chassé, pas failli, and pas de bourrée held an important role in Ponomarev's jump combinations. These movements connect the basic steps and give a rounded wholeness to the entire combination. Some teachers avoid connecting movements in the allegro, preferring to combine the basic steps, but this merely lengthens the students' path to stage variations—the main structural forms of stage dance. There are no variations that consist only of strong jumps and turns; they all presuppose percussive moments and moments of release. An exception, I suppose, is the Blue Bird's variation, which Petipa kept at the top note of the choreographic scale. Flying out over the stage in the first soubresaut, the performer returns to the ground only for the next push off. Consciously violating the model of the academic variation that he himself had created, the ballet master artfully captured the image of a bird's flight in the chain of soubresaut, jeté entrelacé, and entrechat-six.

In the first jump variation created by Ponomarev which young Pushkin noted in 1924, pas de bourrée en tournant follow the assemblé and sparkling entrechat-quatre and entrechat-trois. With the first jumps, the teacher wanted to combine lessons (jump batterie methods and development of plié) with dance skills. The second combination is much more developed than the first, filled with jumps en tournant, and includes dynamic cabrioles with beats as well as tiny beats light as a breeze, brisé. The next movement is more complex—the glissade. Notably, both the first and second combinations contain quite a few small beats. Ponomarev gave virtuoso beats as much attention as flying and powerful jumps or dynamic turns. His graduates could easily master a choreographic text of any complexity.

Nevertheless, the situation in the theater was changing. What suffered most in the stage practice of the 1930s was virtuoso small technique. On the one hand, it contradicted the idea that "heroic dance" was the most important aspect of performance to master. On the other, there was no place for it in the scenarios of choreodramas. In the 1930s and 1940s, virtuoso dance took a backseat to psychological drama. The heroes of ballet dramas got to dance even less than the heroines. Instead, they were expected to give convincing portrayals within the drama of the plot and express the characters' feelings—more often in pantomime than dance. As a result, the gap between the school and the theater grew wider. The school held fast to its standards and continued to train well-rounded, strong dancers. The theater did not use their full potential. Even Sergeyev, as a master of the choreodrama and a subtle psychological actor, complained that in modern productions "there is no dancing at all, or almost none."[33] Chabukiani dreamed of dancing ballets with a central male role that would let him use everything he had learned in ballet school. Not finding anything like them in the works of the masters of choreodrama, he created two ballets with extraordinarily developed choreography for those days: *The Heart of the Hills* (1938) and *Laurencia* (1939). After them, working with Ponomarev, his teacher and a prime connoisseur of the legacy, he revived the old *La Bayadère*, in which he performed the role of Solor, strengthening the dancing while making the character more heroic. However, Chabukiani's ballets were not the rule but the exception in that era of choreodrama's triumphant reign.

Ponomarev understood the tenor of the times, but he did not give up his convictions. He felt that these ephemeral manifestations in ballet would pass and that any truly important contributions would become part of the classical canon. He believed that the future of ballet was in dance.

Choreodrama had to undergo a major internal crisis before it made way for the future of dance, but it was Ponomarev's heir, Pushkin, who would work in the transitional period that culminated with the restoration of dance in ballet, and who would prepare professional dancers for that moment. Pushkin combined in his teaching Johansson's imagination in varying dance steps, Cecchetti's attention to the virtuoso side of performance and physical stamina, Gerdt's preference for smooth transitions from movement to pose and his sense of style, Legat's logic and unity in combinations, and, of course, the profound knowledge of the fundamental principles of executing steps that he had acquired directly from his mentor Ponomarev.

Scrupulously safeguarding the precepts of his predecessors, Pushkin moved into the future.

Nikolai Legat as Jean de Briand in *Raymonda*. The photograph is inscribed to the fifteen-year-old Pushkin: "You, my boy, are Pushkin, while I'm only Legat. 1922. 28 June."

Vladimir Ponomarev. The photograph is inscribed: "To my best student, Sasha Pushkin, to remember Vl. Ponomarev. 3. VI. 1925."

Teacher

CHAPTER 3

The students of Alexander Ivanovich Pushkin have no trouble remembering him as he entered the rehearsal hall.

In autumn and winter he wore a dark suit, white shirt, and monochrome tie. In spring, as if in acknowledgment of nature's holiday and the nearness of final exams, he wore a light gray suit, gray sweater, and the usual white shirt. He moved unhurriedly from the door to the piano, where the accompanist was already seated, bade him a good day, and then, with a welcoming look around the room, he would signal the start of class. Four measures of music sounded slowly and the students lined up along the barre, their heads lowered in a bow. The teacher approached a free barre at the mirror and, with arm raised like an inhalation of air, assigned the first combination of the exercise: "In all positions, two grands pliés, as usual." Class began. After the battements tendus, his suit jacket would be hanging on a chair. By the time the students were in the center, the tie would be loosened and the shirt collar undone. Labor! Every moment was labor, for the students and the teacher alike. Anyone who slipped into class and, entranced, found a place from which to watch the students and teacher realized that this was work. The teacher did not merely lead the class, he created it.

Thirty-eight years of teaching. Thirty-eight years of selfless imparting of knowledge, strength, kindness, and love. Long, marvelous years of faithful service to his art, the art of classical dance.

In a long-standing tradition, begun back in the St. Petersburg Theater School, the classical dance class for upperclassmen is given in the morning. The school's corridors, the monotonous narrow corridors, are usually quiet then. Through the closed doors, the muted sounds of music and the sharp or intentionally slow remarks of the teachers can be heard. You can experience a sense of eternity at moments like these, because life was like this within these walls a century ago, a hundred and fifty years ago, and so on.

Alexander Pushkin in the 1940s.

But near Pushkin's classroom, there often crowded a large group of interested observers. The double doors stood wide open. In the doorway, as if in a theater box, trying not to move so as not to disturb the class and be thrown out, were the lucky ones who had gotten to the front. You could see artists from the theater, students with a free period, guests from the provinces here on their own business. The same phenomenon occurred with his class for the soloists, except the audience was even larger. In his later years of teaching, Pushkin had become famous. What he said, what he assigned as an exercise, and how the students or soloists executed his combinations were all of the greatest interest to ballet professionals.

Yes, the professional level of Pushkin's classes was extremely high. There was much to learn and much to wonder at. But to fully appreciate and understand Pushkin the teacher, you must know him as a person.

Pushkin was not one of those teachers who get results from students through sheer willpower and persistence. He didn't resort to shouts or demands. No one can remember his ever even raising his voice. His tactfulness and gentleness created a teaching atmosphere that put no pressure on the students. "Getting inspired himself during class, he enticed us along with him,"[1] remarked Nikolai Kovmir, one of the last of Pushkin's students, later a soloist of the Maryinsky Theater.

He used not the whip, but inspiration, to make students tirelessly repeat a difficult combination. He sincerely commiserated with his students' failures in class. It would have been so much easier to pour out accumulated impatience than to keep repeating in a quiet voice, "Take it softly, stand taller and push off harder with your left heel. You'll have two turns." The student, upset by his own inability, would get angry and sometimes raise his voice. Then the teacher would shrug in bewilderment and silently go over to his chair. It would grow very quiet in the room. The boy's face would turn red. Pushkin could teach important lessons in the course of his class: how to deal with people, with one's elders; how to appreciate the work of a comrade, a colleague, or a teacher. "It would be hard to find a more sensitive and kind person with both children and adults,"[2] said Nadezhda Bazarova, his partner onstage and a colleague at the school.

He never envied anyone. He could take true pleasure in the success of colleagues in the theater and at the school. During examinations he noted all the positive aspects of a class, all the achievements of both students and teacher. He saw the flaws, of course, but he tried to understand them, to discover the reason for them, knowing how hard it was to teach the art of classical dance. What he disliked most was mindless execution of an assignment—that is, dancing that came about without an understanding of the correct execution of any step. "Where are you twisting yourself to?" he would say, trying to stop a student who had arrived at the class of perfection. "First think where you have to put your leg when doing a double assemblé en tournant, and then start learning the step. Understand the ABC's and only then, without frightening anyone, jump." And, deeply saddened because a young man with good physical attributes for a classical dancer was badly trained, he would assign a combination that was simpler than usual and watch the class attentively but silently.

What seemed as natural as breathing to Pushkin's students seemed new and difficult to those who came to his class from other schools, and often from other countries—difficult not because the combinations required virtuosity, but because the newcomers did not know how to execute the organically connected steps that formed the combinations. I will speak of the combinations later. Now, let me note that Pushkin was sensitive to the mood of the class and tried to maintain the kind of heightened emotional tone he treasured. The atmosphere in his class was amazingly like the calm atmosphere, completely lacking in nervousness, of Ponomarev's classes and the "up" and animated mood of Legat's. Recalling Pushkin's classes, those at school or those for soloists of the theater, I always picture the passion of competition to execute the most complex steps, the joking and laughter. It wasn't a lack of discipline. The class was energized for the rest of the day thanks to Pushkin's lessons.

The theater season of 1967–68. It was impossible to get near the hall where the company's soloists worked. Students and other observers were mesmerized by Vladlen Semenov, always incredibly neat in dress and execution; Yuri Soloviev, focused on something deep within himself; Valery Panov, explosive, ready to respond to a challenge at any moment. Yet even then one stood out, "littlest" nineteen-year-old Mikhail Baryshnikov, perhaps the teacher's favorite, and already the winner of the International Competition in Varna. The end of every class turned into a dance contest. Pushkin went off into a quiet corner and merely indicated changes in tempo to the pianist. Unfortunately for us, no camera ever caught the teacher's eyes at those times. These were moments of triumph, pride, and satisfaction: a brilliant class of soloists composed of graduates from different years and of different teachers at the school, who formed a single unit as a result of Pushkin's work.

Evening. The classes and rehearsals are over. The magnificent Architect Rossi Street, as elegant as the line of the corps de ballet, is empty. No one is hoping for an "extra" ticket for the theater. The flocks of girls and boys from the ballet school have rushed noisily past, headed for the dormitory or their homes. The workday is over for Pushkin, too. Slowly he heads in the direction of Fontanka. His legs and arms are tired. His head is heavy with the sound of his own voice, of the music that has been playing all day. But a student catches up with him, and the teacher's eyes brighten. "You know, you shouldn't spin around meaninglessly. It's better to do fewer turns but cleaner ones." And without a transition, "Have you had dinner? Yes? Then we can walk around a bit." There was nothing he didn't discuss in those evening walks. Pushkin loved his city and knew it well. St. Petersburg—Leningrad. And he tried to tell his students as much as possible about it. It didn't matter whether a boy was going to work there or move to some faraway theater; what mattered was that he retained his love for the great city's beauty.

"I wasn't taught the way you are," he would tell us about the past. The past when the water froze in the watering can in the corner of the rehearsal hall, and when students came to the theater to have lunch with their ration cards (which they received for performing). The teachers were strict and didn't spoil the skinny, pale pupils.

He often recalled Ponomarev. The first year of study went by like a day for Sasha Pushkin. He had fought so long to be accepted by the glorious school! But starting in the second year, he tried to comprehend what he was being taught. "I love studying with him," he wrote in his diary about his teacher. "He gives us new steps every day, we don't stay in one place." It is telling that even in his earliest years at the school, Pushkin was analyzing what he was learning. It would be the cornerstone of his own teaching.

Pushkin took a lot from Ponomarev on how to run a class, beginning with how to provide a creative atmosphere. Perhaps because of his filial loyalty to Ponomarev's precepts, there was something elusively similar between teacher and student. And the more time passed, the more these two marvelous men seemed to share traits in common.

Like Ponomarev, Pushkin was sensitive to the psychological fragility of his students. Canadian dancer David Holmes expressed an important concept in an interview in *Dance and Dancers*. Holmes and his wife and partner,

Anna-Maria Holmes, were interning at the Kirov Theater and the Choreographic School with Pushkin and Natalya Dudinskaya. After his first class with Pushkin, Holmes wanted to go back to Canada, because he realized that he wasn't prepared even to do the exercises at the barre (and yet he was a soloist in the Winnipeg Royal Ballet!). But the teacher's kindness filled him with self-confidence, and diligent work brought quick, positive results. For the first two weeks, Pushkin made no remarks about the newcomer's work; only when he sensed that Holmes was more comfortable in the class did he begin giving careful, brief bits of advice to help him through the "labyrinths" of combinations and point out his mistakes in execution: the real "Pushkinian" work had begun. That's why, when asked what he considered the most important part of the Kirov teachers' method, Holmes replied, "The capacity I've found all really great teachers have—and that's patience. That gentle approach, a way of encouraging. Pushkin has it, Dudinskaya has it, Shelest has it and Messerer at the Bolshoi has it."[3]

Encouragement was, indeed, characteristic of Pushkin's style. He always tried to find the words to restore a student's strength, to keep the fire burning in his eyes throughout a class or a rehearsal. "Don't rush the approach. Calm down. We're going to repeat the whole thing, and you mustn't think about the beat, just push off from the deep plié and look at point 8." The teacher's tone was encouraging, and the rehearsal went on.

Holmes's success after studying with Pushkin was described in a letter to the Pushkin family by another of his students, Voytek Veselovski, a dancer from Warsaw: "Now we can see what great strides he made, thanks to you."[4]

Pushkin had many students from other countries. "Too bad that you can't see all your former students who are now all over the world,"[5] wrote Egon Bischoff from

Alexander Pushkin and his wife, Xenia Yurgenson.

Alexander Pushkin and Rudolf Nureyev.

Berlin in October 1961. Those words could have been a painful reminder. Just four months before this letter was written, his favorite student, Rudolf Nureyev, had made his "most famous jump."

Many things bound pupil and teacher together. Nureyev, who had come from Ufa, where he had mastered the rudiments of dance and had even performed in the local theater, spent three years in Pushkin's class. Exceptionally gifted but impulsive, abrupt, and with an uncontrollable temper, he was an object of pride and at the same time a source of constant anxiety for the teacher. And almost immediately after graduation from the school—in 1958, newly accepted into the theater's company—Nureyev ended up living with the Pushkin family. The reason for the invitation was an injury he received during a rehearsal of *Laurencia*; the doctors recommended a special regimen and diet. Pushkin made an instant decision, which had actually been brewing for a while. But you must understand the living conditions of the celebrated ballet teacher. The Pushkins—Alexander Ivanovich and his wife, artist of the theater Xenia Iosifovna Yurgenson—had one room in a communal flat in the same building on Architect Rossi Street as the school itself. And in that room, crowded with ancient wood furniture, there appeared a cot where Rudik slept—in the mornings, the cot was hidden behind a screen. But life here was imbued with art and subsumed by it. Endless discussions of rehearsals and performances, tales of famous dancers of the past, socializing with present-day ballet stars, and an atmosphere of kindness and hospitality made up the aura of the Pushkin home.

Rudolf absorbed it all like a sponge. Going to the Philharmonic, attending premieres at the drama theater and art exhibits, and taking trips with his teacher to palaces and parks outside the city must have left an indelible mark on the young artist. He was not spoiled, he was being trained in the strict discipline a ballet soloist requires, yet at the same time he was surrounded by paternal love and care.

Nureyev lived with the Pushkins right up until his departure for Paris in the summer of 1961. He didn't return from the tour, and Pushkin never saw him again—neither at home, in the rehearsal hall, nor onstage. Infrequent bits of news, magazines, and photographs that reached his house by mysterious routes were all that was left for the teacher. Rudik never forgot the Pushkins' birthdays and he always called at New Year's. Abroad, there was success and world fame; here, on Architect Rossi Street, Pushkin never expressed his feelings to anyone. The severe illness that felled him in 1962 was undoubtedly brought on by the inner tension of the previous months. He didn't feel isolated or persecuted. He wasn't very bothered by the disappearance of people once close to the family; that was to be expected in those days. Much worse was the thought that Rudik would never again appear in that room and that they would never again go together to a dance lesson or rehearsal. Living with that knowledge was not easy. Pushkin had a long and difficult convalescence, but his pupils were waiting for him in class. He maintained his former demeanor with them—that is, he was kind and attentive—but he never allowed anyone into his heart again.

Many people, even colleagues in the company who had observed him over long years of teaching, could not understand how this modest man, so taciturn in public, who had never attempted to clothe his knowledge in literary language, could inculcate in his students the joy of dance, a passionate thirst for a full-blooded life on the stage and a profound interest in culture and art in the broadest sense of the word. He did it by giving them his heart and his own inexhaustible love for dance and culture.

"My dear Alexander Ivanovich," wrote Gelu Barbu, one of Romania's finest dancers, "you will always be my best memory, I will always be grateful for the fact that it was you alone who turned me into a dancer.... When Lavrovsky handed me the diploma and medal as laureate of the International Competition in Warsaw, I thought of you. I thought of you a lot and thanked you for everything you have given me. You cannot imagine how I appreciate you and love you, my only teacher!"[6]

Yes, Pushkin knew how to "make" dancers, just as he knew how to teach them to work without stinting. That moral law was inviolable for Pushkin the pupil and Pushkin the performer, and it became the most important one for Pushkin the teacher.

We have before us the record book for Ponomarev's class for the 1924–25 school year. In six months, Pushkin was absent only once. And he instilled in his own pupils the same loyalty to the art of ballet. He understood that you could get tired or become ill, but he didn't understand the words "not in the mood" or "don't want to." As far as he was concerned, dance and laziness, dance and capriciousness, were not compatible.

Did Pushkin know Dobrolyubov's words? "The educator's obligation consists in making himself superfluous as soon as possible, training the child to understand moral law in its true essence, independent of the educator's authority."[7]

He avoided moralistic words, affirming moral law by the way he lived his life. It is impossible to forget how embarrassing Alexander Ivanovich found applause and flowers. I'll never forget what he used to say: "I can't go out on the street with flowers! Let's give them to the women." All the flowers given to the teacher were handed out to the accompanists and pupils. Pushkin did everything so naturally that it was impossible to refuse him. I remember how he turned pale, doing his exercises at the barre, when he was told of the death of the father of one of his students. He treasured every pupil, his life was filled with concern for everyone who stood before him in class. He became their support, sharing their woes and joys. And his students, leaving the school, always preserved their feeling of trust in the man who had given them their professional knowledge. The deepest secrets were revealed to the teacher, and every student was certain of being understood, of hearing the right words, and—if at all possible—of being given help.

Communication with his charges and care for them didn't end with graduation; it continued for many years. Even if he lost direct touch with some of his former students, invisible threads connected them. Back in 1935 (Pushkin's first graduating class), Leonid Oshurko completed the evening courses. At the graduation concert he danced the pas de deux from *The Sleeping Beauty*, which he had prepared with the young teacher. Fate separated them for many years. Oshurko worked in the provinces, moving around a lot, and specializing in folk dance (he is the author of *Folk Dances of Moldavia* [Kishinev, 1957]). But forty years later, Pushkin's first student would write, "Yet again I must say: I owe a lot to Alexander Ivanovich Pushkin for my growth in the arts. He had kind hands, which directed us into life and into art."[8] Much more frequently, though, he maintained very close ties with his former pupils.

Pushkin's class. An ordinary lesson. Forgetting everything else in the world, concentrating, the pupils perform combinations. In the center of the hall, groups change. First, second, third, then first again. Tirelessly, they do developpé, demi-plié, fouetté en tournant.... And suddenly: "Don't lift your leg higher than 45 degrees! You'll have time for that in the theater. But for now, check everything, polish every movement, every position!" To whom are these words addressed? The class is supposed to be for students only. But no, at Alexander Ivanovich's class there was usually a performer practicing as well, one of his former students. It could be someone who had graduated long ago, who had been working in a theater for many years, or it could be someone who had graduated the previous year and had come back to his teacher to prepare his first major role.

The lesson ends, and the teacher stays on. "Well, come on. You know the order, don't you? Let's begin." And they begin work on Siegfried, which the teacher may never see on stage. But here, in the rehearsal hall, they will find something that the young dancer will take back home 1,000 kilometers away. And after his debut, he will write to his teacher about the performance and its reviews, receiving a response with the laconic but important lines: "Congratulations on the premiere of *Swan Lake*. I'm very pleased: continue perfecting your mastery."[9] Even here Pushkin does not forget to remind his pupils of the most important thing: you cannot stop, you must "continue perfecting your mastery." And then he adds his news: "April 30 we had our examinations. They went well." Another moral lesson. The words "went well" refer to the applause of the theater's famous dancers, the State Examination Commission, the pupils in the audience who filled the upper gallery of the rehearsal hall. It was his way of telling his pupil: applause, flowers—that's not the main thing. What's important is what life will hold both for you and for my students who just passed their graduation exams today. This is what you should be thinking about, for a life in art is an endless examination.

In his draft notebooks containing hundreds of combinations, we can find brief appraisals of his students, and his words are interesting because they indicate the growth potential of each dancer. "Emets. Good attributes. A bit too slow. Good jump and turn. Can be used as a classical dancer." Time confirmed that conclusion, reached in 1967: Valery Emets became an interesting classical dancer. His repertoire included not only the virtuoso duet from *Don Quixote* and the pas de trois in *Swan Lake*, but also Herman in Boyarschikov's one-act ballet *The Queen of Spades*, which in its time was a sensation, and the solo role in *Ballet Divertissement*, choreographed by Georgiy Aleksidze to music by Mozart. The teacher had prepared his student for a career onstage as a soloist.

About Vladimir Fedyanin, Pushkin wrote: "Good attributes. With temperament. Can perform solo parts." When he came to the theater, Fedyanin immediately became a soloist, distinguished by his polished technique, emotionality, and expressiveness; his good qualities shone particularly in the pas de deux from *Flames of Paris*. Illness kept Fedyanin from taking the graduation examination with his class (1967), and he was left back for a year, but he didn't return to his teacher (even though Pushkin taught the class of perfection), switching to B. Ya. Bregvadze, with whom he completed his studies. Once he joined the Kirov Ballet, Fedyanin once again started studying in Pushkin's class. Did Pushkin feel any hurt over his "unfaithful" student? No, he understood the questing temperament of this youth. He realized that Fedyanin was trying to find himself and seeking among various teachers something that responded to his individuality. Moreover, Pushkin sensed that this student was drawn to the unusual and tried to help him find his place in art. And he was right. A few years later, Fedyanin left the Kirov in order to work in Odessa with the interesting choreographer I. Chernyshev. There he danced the Prince in Chernyshev's *The Nutcracker* and Basil in *Don Quixote*, in which he was unexpectedly controlled and graphic in every pose of his original interpretation of the pas de deux. Fedyanin also danced the part of the Kurd in Alexei Chichinadze's choreographic poem *Gayane*. The choreographer used Fedyanin's natural gifts in creating the Kurd's dance: powerful push off, sharpness of legs in executing large jumps, and an infectious passion. As performed by Fedyanin, this dance became the focal point of the ballet. Pushkin had determined precisely in which roles Fedyanin would have the greatest success. Later,

Rudolf Nureyev as Frondoso in *Laurencia*, Kirov Theater.

Rudolf Nureyev in the pas de deux from *Le Corsaire*, Covent Garden.

Fedyanin's indefatigable spirits led him, a laureate of the International Competition in Varna, to the Komische Opera in Berlin to work with the choreographer T. Schilling.

I wonder what Pushkin would have written about Nureyev, if he had recorded his thoughts in the late 1950s. "Naturally gifted dancer. Must work on his 'schooling.' But what a unique talent." Naturally, Pushkin foresaw Nureyev's brilliant future, but he knew his weaknesses, too; after all, Nureyev came to his class as a seventeen year old. And Pushkin the teacher demanded perfection in everything—from the simplest elementary dance to the peaks of virtuoso dancing.

There exists a rare film shot in the late 1950s. Nureyev is rehearsing the Prince's variation from *The Nutcracker*. You won't often see such an unexpected and aesthetically unique performance. Slightly lowered arm position, sharp instantaneous stops, in which the arrow-like tautness of the lift is underlined by the pose of the head and hands. A piano accompanies, but the dance seems to embody the sounds of an orchestra. Sissonne tombée, sissonne and a leap into saut de basque—this combination was performed around in a circle, softly, like a cat, but with unusual dynamism. And yet the shoulders and torso remain absolutely still. Only in Nureyev's performance of the second part of the Prince's variation in Vainonen's choreography is the dancing appropriate to the music. The emotional and technical explosion of the dance responds to the orchestra's forte. Pushkin was always with Nureyev when he prepared his roles: the Prince in *The Nutcracker* and *Sleeping Beauty*, Basil and Frondoso, Count Albrecht....

It was the summer of 1969. The Bolshoi Theater. The First Moscow International Ballet Competition. Pushkin was walking down the corridor, extremely agitated. Unexpectedly, seeing a familiar face, he said without preamble: "Misha's knee still hurts!" Yet when the competition was over,

Olga Moiseyeva as Nikia, and Rudolf Nureyev as Solor, in *La Bayadère*, Kirov Theater.

Irina Kolpakova as Giselle, and Rudolf Nureyev as Count Albrecht, in *Giselle*, Kirov Theater.

Rudolf Nureyev in the title role of *Hamlet*, Covent Garden.

Mikhail Baryshnikov, his pride, had won the gold medal.

He had appeared in Pushkin's class in 1964, arriving from Riga, where he had studied with a good teacher, Juris Kapralis. Coming home elatedly after an audition, Pushkin announced that he had accepted a marvelous pupil. Xenia Iosifovna, with a touch of mocking jealousy, asked, "What, better than Rudik?" Pushkin thought and replied seriously, "He is completely different, but no less talented." People started talking about the young dancer soon afterward, first at school, then in the theater, then throughout the country, and then all over the ballet world.

Mercurial, childlike in appearance, with wide-open blue eyes, yet the embodiment of inner concentration and discipline in his work, he melted Pushkin's heart from the start. Misha soon became a daily visitor at his teacher's home. By that time, the family had gotten a second room. Alexander Ivanovich liked working there, making his notations, checking movements and combinations in the mirror, often going over them with Misha's help. And once more there were walks in the city with visits to the Strelka, the islands; once again conversation about the art of ballet, its glorious past, and its masters. Alexander Ivanovich had a great sense of humor and was an amusing raconteur, and Misha, receptive and witty, was a worthy partner. At that time the young Baryshnikov was entranced by songs by the bards and sang a bit and played the guitar. Alexander Ivanovich liked listening to him and sometimes sang along. The relationship between pupil and teacher was uncommonly harmonious, helped by Misha's intelligence and culture and his profound loyalty to Pushkin.

He was always nearby. At the time, I was working with Pushkin before an important appearance in *Swan Lake*, and I remember how terribly angered Baryshnikov was by the "stupidity" of his recent classmate, who couldn't get the musicality of the second part of the Prince's variation.

Pushkin stopped the irate "premier" and with a sly smile in grumpy Baryshnikov's direction calmly demonstrated yet again how to execute the complicated musical phrase. And Baryshnikov was there once again, forgetting the "insult," immediately demonstrating yet another variant, which might be more suitable to the individuality of the debuting dancer. Alexander Ivanovich created an atmosphere that was at once free and demanding, kind and uncompromising, and which was supported by his students. And that didn't depend on the place where we worked, our titles or measure of talent. We were all Pushkin's students.

Of course, Baryshnikov held a special place among that "all." Very quickly, almost as soon as he first appeared on the stage in 1967, he took the place of a premier, which was commensurate with his talent, but he also achieved creative maturity in his very first leading roles—Basil, Mercutio in *Romeo and Juliet*, Adam in *Creation of the World*, and especially Albrecht in *Giselle*—which was a much rarer phenomenon. As for his dancing, he embodied Pushkin's dream of perfection. Every step Baryshnikov executed reflected perfection. In that sense, Baryshnikov's polished dancing was not only Pushkin's greatest creation, but also the highest accolade to Pushkin's service and devotion to ballet, to his life and all his work.

Pushkin was wholeheartedly devoted to Baryshnikov and, having already suffered one painful loss, feared losing him as well. According to a friend of Pushkin's, this sometimes took on a somewhat comical aspect. The teacher protected the young dancer from personal contacts with foreigners. If one of his former foreign students dropped by to see Alexander Ivanovich when Baryshnikov was present, the young dancer was ushered into the next room on some pretext and kept there until the guest left. And the guest might not have been any more foreign than a Pole or East German![10]

Top: Alexander Pushkin with graduates from the Choreographic School. Left to right: Alexander Pushkin, Vladimir Fedyanin, Mikhail Baryshnikov, Alexander Bruskin, Sergei Fedyanin.

Mikhail Baryshnikov and Alexander Pushkin.

Alexander Pushkin in the class for soloists of the theater, 1969. In foreground, Mikhail Baryshnikov.

Graduation examination in Pushkin's class, 1967. In foreground, Mikhail Baryshnikov.

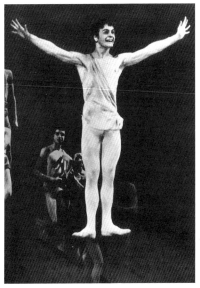 

Mikhail Baryshnikov as Adam in *Creation of the World*, Kirov Theater.

Mikhail Baryshnikov as Daphnis in *Daphnis and Chloe*, Baryshnikov Celebration at the Kirov Theater.

Alas, Baryshnikov, like Nureyev, was also lost to Russia. But before that happened, he was with his teacher when he died, and although only twenty-two years old, he brought the orphaned Pushkin class to graduation.

When Pushkin first grew terribly ill and the doctors told him to stop teaching in order to preserve his health, he replied with his usual shrug: "Better to die in the classroom than to live in bed." He could not imagine himself without his beloved work. And so things continued in the orderly way of so many years: the soloists' class at the theater, the class at the school, rehearsals with students. He could be seen every day slowly walking along Architect Rossi Street with a radiantly joyful look of anticipation on his face. Pushkin was on his way to his students.

The teacher's habits didn't change even when his heart began acting up. As usual, he approached the barre by the mirror and would lightly "sketch out the text" of a new combination. Of course, after his serious illness Pushkin extended his vacation, which coincided with the vacation at the theater. The students had to start their school year with another teacher, and they waited impatiently to hear news from where their teacher was resting. The Baltic Sea, where Pushkin usually vacationed, gave him new strength. Looking younger, longing for work, he would return to the ballet classroom. And then there would be more work, and more, and more. Once again, although he would not pay attention to the time during the class, he always got his entire lesson completed.

All the rules and habits remained in force. In the 1950s, the Pushkins had established a tradition: three times a year, the entire class came to visit. The visits were in September, for his birthday (the date varied with the start of the school year); before New Year's, on December 30; and in late April after the final exams. They came with flowers and with simple, boyish presents. They shyly crowded into the

Victor Rona as Basil in *Don Quixote*, Hungarian Opera Theater. Intern, 1959.

Sergei Berezhnoi as Prince Charming in *The Sleeping Beauty*, Kirov Theater. Graduate, 1970.

T.-C. Kremke performing with the German State Opera. Intern, 1963.

Valery Emets as Gennaro in *Napoli*, Kirov Theater. Graduate, 1967.

Alexander Pushkin in a class of
perfection, 1968–69 school year.

Alexander Pushkin with the class of perfection, 1968–69 school year. His last graduating class. Standing, left to right: Vladimir Soldatenko, Nikolai Kovmir, Sergei Berezhnoi, Vladimir Bondarenko, Alexander Pushkin, V. Sergeyev, Arstan Irsaliev, Maki Homura (intern from Japan), Jean Oubier (intern from Belgium), V. Sychev. Seated, left to right: Semyon Lapin, Vitaly Firsov, Yuri Zubarev.

entry hall. The hosts' geniality and hospitality relaxed them. They sat down with jokes and stories at the beautiful table set with homemade foods. At New Year's—as an exception—one bottle of champagne was offered for all of them. The table, under a starched cloth, with silverware, crystal dishes, and shimmering candles, seemed like something out of a magical fairy tale to the boys. Many of them lived in the dormitory, far from family and home, and probably most of them had never seen anything like it. At dinner, Alexander Ivanovich tried to chat with each one, not overlooking anyone, giving advice along the way, and making jokes. In the spring, after exams, they discussed all the performances in a kind and merry way. And Xenia Iosifovna bustled about, trying to fill up plates, especially for the pale and skinny lads.

But the teacher's days were numbered.

It was 1968. The class of perfection. There were students present from various schools around the country. Of course, they could jump high and do eight or even ten pirouettes, but Pushkin wanted something else. He wanted the jump to be expressive, plastic, graphic in form, the knees not stretched, the wrists free, and the head turned at an angle that was harmonious with the torso. "Let's repeat the combination. Redjep, you're not at the gates of Pakhtakor. Please, control the temperament and remember the landing after the jeté." And once again, the students shot out in a jeté, soubresaut, pas failli, trying to retain the necessary position in the air and not thump on landing. At the end of the class, each would go through excerpts of variations that the teacher had selected for him. Redjep Abdyev, then a graduate of the Tashkent Choreographic School, would demonstrate his big jump in the coda from *Swan Lake*. He would soon become a soloist with the Maly Opera Theater and then the Kirov Theater, where he would dance the parts of Basil, Frondoso, Solor, Ali-Batyr, and Ferkhad, leading roles in a varied repertoire.

Victor Garapes as Prince Siegfried in *Swan Lake*, Prague National Theater. Intern, 1969.

Hans Meister as Spartacus in *Spartacus*, Zurich Opera Theater. Intern, 1970.

Vadim Budarin as Basil in
Don Quixote, Kirov Theater.
Graduate, 1961.

Redjep Abdyev as Solor in
La Bayadère, Kirov Theater.
Graduate, 1968.

It was 1969. We are looking at a snapshot. The class in fifth position. The teacher stands surrounded by his students. A marvelous feel for épaulement, extended knees, light arms. You can almost hear: "Pull back your shoulder blades. Hands softer. Elbows, elbows. Well, come on now." The class is in session. Pushkin assigns a combination. "Second arabesque. Head to the audience. Bring the leg out of the arabesque into à la seconde and quickly turn into effacée."

That was the last class Pushkin trained.

The final months of his life were darkened by a problem that he could not solve. The Kirov Theater had managed to build new rehearsal rooms, expanding the walls of its building. The dancers were now able to do their exercises right in the theater and then move directly into rehearsals; previously, the artists of the ballet had always practiced in the same rooms on Architect Rossi Street that in the morning were filled by the children of the choreographic school—to the great joy of the adolescents, who could watch the great masters in person. Once the artists left, one of the most important arteries connecting the school and the theater was severed.

This was a personal disaster for Pushkin. His health didn't permit him to travel first to Theater Square and then to Architect Rossi Street. He wanted the leading soloists to go on studying in the school building, but that made the new set-up useless. His favorite adult students were leaving, yet he couldn't imagine life without them, just as, when he was a child, he couldn't imagine himself without ballet. The dancers knew how acutely Pushkin felt the coming separation, but to everyone's great regret, no way out of the situation could be found. The thread tying his life to the life of his students, his fledglings, in the theater that was most dear to him, was about to break. But it was his life that broke off instead.

It was evening, an ordinary evening on Architect Rossi Street. Rehearsals in Pushkin's graduating class were coming to an end. They were looking for the best variant of the variation in the pas de deux from *Le Corsaire*. Nikolai Kovmir was rehearsing. Pushkin proposed that the graduating student replace the jeté en tournant with double tours en l'air in first arabesque. Kovmir had his doubts. "In the coda you'll do the jeté, Kolya, and the variation will be improved by the doubles," Pushkin persuaded him gently. At the graduation concert, after his teacher's death, the student obeyed his command, but that evening they didn't reach agreement and said goodnight until the next day as usual. Leaving the school, Pushkin ran into a recent graduate, Larisa Ermolova, a friend of his and Xenia's. They had a brief chat, a hurried discussion about her problems starting out on her career. He said a few kind words. And they parted.

He died of a heart attack on the street, on the way home from the ballet school.

Pushkin's School

CHAPTER 4

Pushkin himself always considered his classes labor. In his students' eyes, they were art. "It cannot be called work, it was Creation,"[1] wrote yet another of Pushkin's students, German Yanson. Yes, for the students they were unforgettable hours of communion with art—hours that taught them how to achieve their goals, hours that inspired their creative quest.

Nevertheless, not everyone who had the good fortune to study in his class or was a colleague at the school got used to Pushkin's "scattering" of combinations and his succinct, extremely concrete comments. And first-time visitors to his class, both other teachers and artists, were always amazed.

In December 1967, John Barker, head of a ballet school in New York, visited Pushkin's class. What he saw made him "study Russian so I could talk to him and to learn from him how to be a better teacher,"[2] as he wrote two years later. He was astonished by the combinations of steps assigned to the students and the atmosphere of the class. "Only now do I understand how much energy I wasted flying into occasional rages,"[3] Barker wrote to Pushkin in 1968.

Mikhail Mikhailov, who had taught for many years at the school, recalled that it was quite common in the 1960s for the school to be visited by foreign choreographers, ballet artists, ballet scholars and critics, and teachers. The first request made by guests was almost always the same, "Professor Pushkin class, please!"[4]

Pushkin was generous and had no professional secrets. Thousands of combinations of steps were written down in composition books now to be found on the desks of dancers and teachers in various corners of the world. Pushkin allowed people to take notes in his class—it was natural to him to do anything that could help his beloved art. That's why he sent his notes on *Chopiniana* and *Giselle* to chief ballet master Miroslav Kura in Brno (also a former student), and that's why people from Riga and Tashkent, Berlin and

Nikolai Kovmir as Frondoso in
Laurencia, Kirov Theater.
Graduate, 1970.

Top: Anna-Maria and David Holmes in *Melody by Gluck*, Winnipeg Royal Ballet, Canada. Interns, 1968.

Vyacheslav Maimusov in *Le Sacre du Printemps*, Estonia Theater. Graduate, 1967.

Sofia, Ottawa and New York, asked him for help. Everyone knew that Pushkin would respond and help in every way he could.

The class is considered the foundation of the art of ballet. It is in class that dancers begin to learn the basics of dancing onstage. It is class that develops and supports the technical, physical, and artistic form of dancers, and knowing how to combine these three elements is what distinguishes the truly talented teacher. Pushkin was a master of all three aspects of the art of pedagogy. His methodology intertwined them organically in the structure of his class. From the first movements at the barre to the classical variations that crowned every class, there was a harmonious and logical progression to the professional tasks set by the teacher, whose students acquired a mastery of the technique of dance and developed their physical strength while being taught not to "work" but to dance. Nikita Dolgushin, a brilliant dancer who is head of the choreography department at the St. Petersburg Conservatory, described Pushkin's class this way: "Just lasting through his entire class and fulfilling at least the minimal requirements was already proof of the artist's high professional level."[5]

Pushkin's internal metronome didn't let him alter the tried-and-true rhythm of the class. This rhythm was an essential part of his methodology, yet the impression he created was that he was unhurried, even a bit slow in demonstrating each movement. But this was the best rhythm for students to learn the order of steps in a combination, something very important for the success of the lesson. If a student confuses the order of steps, he loses the ability to execute the full exercise. This could not happen in Pushkin's class. He didn't orient himself solely on the class "leader"— and this was yet another important aspect of the man—but took into consideration the abilities of the class as a whole.

Yes, Pushkin made few remarks—in fact, he was taciturn during class—but the combinations he assigned spoke for him in developing both technique and dance ability. This was the basis of his method, a manifestation of his talent, experience, and care for his students. Preparing for class—and numerous accounts show this—Pushkin assiduously created combinations that addressed their needs. In assigning certain linked movements, he conditioned coordination, sense of pose, stability, and many other aspects of classical dance.

In just a few months of working in his class, students acquired a new and more perfect form of movement. A more confident quality appeared in their épaulement; and the arms seemed to assume the correct port de bras at push-off during a jump instead of flailing randomly. The class helped students to overcome sloppiness in their dancing. It healed dancers literally, too, helping them regain physical and technical form after an illness or injury.

Let us study one of the fundamental principles of Pushkin's methodology through a specific case.

In 1968, after a severe injury, Vadim Budarin, a soloist at the Kirov and a former student of Pushkin's (he had graduated from the school in 1961), joined the class of perfection. He had not danced in a long time and began very cautiously. Pushkin made no comments. He would assign a combination, sometimes correcting an unfortunate pose, explain the principle of execution of the steps, and then might say to Budarin, almost casually, "Look for the axis." And Budarin would carefully complete the preparation for the tours, not yet doing the actual turn, still testing his stability and coordination. Watching him, Pushkin could see that the most important thing was to restore his coordination, elasticity, flexibility, and stamina, and he tried to help him concentrate on these aspects of performing. In doing the assigned combinations, the dancer was allowed to simplify

Alexander Pushkin at rehearsal with Svetlana Lisina and Timofei Babanov, 1930s.

their technical side. If the combination included turns, he did a relevé in the assigned position and stood on half-toe while the rest of the class did the turns. In this way he regained his lost sense of stability. In simplifying Pushkin's combinations, the dancer unexpectedly discovered the profound goals hidden in the virtuoso combination of steps.

Removing the ornamentation from a piece of architecture will reveal its structure and foundation. This was the principle of work Pushkin proposed for Budarin, stripping the combinations of their ornaments and revealing their basic goals. He revealed the "seed" of every combination.

Battement fondu in the center: this movement prepares the muscles for soft landings after jumps.

Battement fondu with right leg to the side at 45 degrees, battement fondu in attitude croisée (right leg at 90 degrees), lower leg into fourth position, pirouettes en dehors in attitude, ending in attitude croisée (Budarin didn't do the pirouettes, merely relevé in the pose). Demi-plié and renversé, pas de bourrée in fourth position, right leg in front. And pirouettes en dedans, ending in attitude effacée (Budarin replaced the pirouette here too with a relevé). And then all over again with the other leg.

At first, it might seem strange that Pushkin proposed a combination in which the main step appears only twice. But that was the strength of Pushkin the teacher: he knew how to combine various steps in such a way that together they solved the problem of the basic movement. Battement fondu develops the demi-plié and stability, which require a strong calf muscle and elastic Achilles' heel. There are only two battements fondu (to the side at 45 degrees and in attitude croisée at 90 degrees), but let's look at how many movements the dancer has done to develop the necessary muscles, even without doing pirouettes. Twice in the combination there are pirouettes in the attitude pose; the accompanying demi-plié and relevé are two more movements

Alexander Pushkin in class, 1940s.

for the development of the calf muscle and stability. Demi-plié, renversé, pas de bourrée—another three movements that use the main working muscle in a battement fondu. As a result, there are seven movements that are either a battement fondu in its complete form or one of its phases (bending or straightening the knee and rising on half-toe). In addition, Budarin stood on half-toe while the rest of the class did the turns, so that he could continue the rest of the combination with them. Thus, there was much attention to the development of stability as well. Even with the technical and dancing difficulties removed (which is why the Budarin example was selected), the combination achieved the main goal of using battement fondu.

Let us not forget that the students were performing a more complex level of the combination than Budarin was. Pushkin brought many valuable things to a combination other than achieving its main goal, which was determined by its basic movement—in this case, the battement fondu. Thus, while working on turning in large poses, he added work on the arms during the transition from one pose to another; throughout the exercises Pushkin devoted a great deal of attention to the arms, seeing them as the key to dance achievement. "The arms must sing during a movement," he often said in class. In other words, Pushkin went beyond the main goal by introducing additional elements that were appropriate for that particular class.

In the next combination—grands battements jetés—there will be pirouettes, but in other poses, there will be the renversé again, at another angle and with different arm position. These lessons made us work not only our bodies but our minds. At a Pushkin class, the dancer tested his abilities to the fullest extent. No wonder Nikita Dolgushin claims that after a Pushkin class you could often skip rehearsal, as opposed, say, to the classes of Asaf Messerer, who usually made the technical goal of each lesson very specific.[6] In one class, Pushkin covered a large number of varied steps and introduced variations from the classical repertoire into the allegro. His students in just a short period executed a heavy physical, technical, and dancing load. How did he do this? Through the tempo of the class, the internal metronome to which I have alluded. The intensity was extreme. The dancer had to think actively and fast, grasping the order of the movements, each of which was logically based on the preceding one.

A focused artist could prepare for a stage performance during such classes. Pushkin sometimes suggested to his best students on the eve of a major performance (I am referring to leading roles) that they work in class in the manner of the coming production, adding a certain stylistic color to the exercise. Without violating the academic rules of executing the ballet steps, Pushkin gave each person the opportunity to manifest individual qualities. That may be why Kasyan Goleizovsky wrote, "I came to fully appreciate Vasiliev's creative power and the harmony of his consistently well considered dance gestures in the class of teacher Pushkin."[7] Naturally, Vasiliev, like Dolgushin, had an instant grasp of the order of steps and the inner essence of a combination, and he tried to give full expression to the creative possibilities in each exercise. Thus, the first adagio in the center was especially reflective of Dolgushin's individuality, since Pushkin built it on soft battements développés, tours lents, fouettés, and ports de bras. In that adagio the dancer could test the beauty of his arabesque, finding an expressive arm position in the transition from one pose to another. The second adagio, which incorporated dynamic turns, sharp poses, and even one or two jumps, indisputably echoed Vasiliev's creative gifts.

Vasiliev and Dolgushin, such different and major creative individuals! The first was trained by Mikhail Gabovich, a famous dancer of the Bolshoi Theater and teacher

Alexander Pushkin in class, 1950s.

at the Moscow Choreographic School; the second graduated from the Leningrad School in Valentin Shelkov's class. But both of them found the important things they needed in Pushkin's class. That is why Goleizovsky placed such value on Vasiliev's encounters with Pushkin, and it is for the same reason that Dolgushin treasures his memories of Pushkin.

"You must go see *Giselle* today. Nikita is back. Go see it. He does everything in his own way," Pushkin told his students when Dolgushin returned to the Kirov stage as Albrecht after a long hiatus. Because Pushkin was so devoted to the highest traditions of Russian ballet, he held independent creative personalities in great esteem. What he saw in Dolgushin was a searching, creatively obsessed artist, capable of rethinking the roles of the classical repertoire seriously and in his own way, and Pushkin had always respected and welcomed this kind of creative artist.

Less than ten years earlier, Rudolf Nureyev had appeared on that stage in the same ballet. It was in Pushkin's class that teacher and pupil found and rehearsed those things that made the young dancer an instant idol of audiences and professionals.

More years passed, and Mikhail Baryshnikov appeared in *Giselle* with his own interpretation of the traditional role. "Then there was ... the magical performance of *Giselle*, which is bound to enter history next to Nijinsky's last St. Petersburg *Giselle*,"[8] wrote Krasovskaya. And Pushkin was there for Baryshnikov, too.

Pushkin determined the strongest points of every student and tried to show him to best advantage in every role. In order to achieve that, he occasionally deviated from the canon. The variation of the White Slave in *Le Pavillon d'Armide*, staged by Fokine especially for Nijinsky, is known for its very difficult first section. Nijinsky, with his phenomenal leaps, did a simple grand changement de pieds while moving from the center of the stage to the right and left.

He could fly over half the stage, reaching an enormous height, in one jump. One student who was preparing that variation for his graduation concert was in great difficulty, since he lacked the qualities needed to be effective in the role; he had been selected to do it because his partner was very good at the adagio and her variation, and he had to support her. Pushkin could see how the poor boy was suffering. "We'll try a different coda today," he said at one rehearsal, and showed him what he had come up with. The student brightened noticeably. And then they found another approach to the tricky first part of the variation: the grand changement de pieds was replaced by an entrechat-six with movement from side to side. The general outline of the dance was preserved, but the beats were unusual, and that allowed the student to overcome his worry and even to some degree to reveal his abilities in the concert.

"Pushkin never repressed a student's individuality," M. M. Mikhailov recalled. "On the contrary, he gave each one his wings to freely explore his own creative impulses. This is why his work was crowned with such extraordinary results. Naturally, the ones who felt freest in expressing their individuality were those who were most talented."[9]

Beginning with that very first class, all of Pushkin's students felt his concern and interest in their person and talent, no matter how modest it might have been. "Alexander Ivanovich was distinguished ... by his profound attention to each of us, which led to his individual approach to every student. I felt it myself. He awakened in each of us our hidden qualities and helped them develop," wrote Leonid Oshurko, Pushkin's first student, in a letter cited above. And yet, it was not clear until the early 1950s that the school had an outstanding master among its teachers. Until then, he was perceived merely as one of the heirs and successors of the school of dancing personified by Ponomarev and, of course, Vaganova.

Alexander Pushkin rehearsing
with Nikolai Kovmir.

At the beginning, Pushkin didn't try to introduce any innovations into his pedagogy. On the contrary, he revered the experience of his mentors. He had had the good fortune to encounter Vaganova before she had been fully appreciated by the school as an exceptionally talented teacher. Attending her class in the summer of 1921 left its mark on the young dancer; even then he was distinguished by a serious and thoughtful approach to his studies. Later, he encountered Vaganova again, as a graduate, when he danced with her students Elena Tangieva and Marina Semenova. Vaganova's influence on male dancers and their teachers was not limited to direct creative work with them. Although she never taught men (except for occasional private lessons), it is impossible to ignore the effect of her pedagogic principles both on the teaching and performance of men.

When we spoke of the structure of Ponomarev's class, we remarked on its connection with her methods. Most significantly, Vaganova formulated in theory and proved in practice essential principles of executing poses and movements in classical dance, principles that applied equally to women and men. As a result, this development of the methodology of dance led to a mutually enhancing and enriching experience for both men and women at the school. Once he became a teacher, Pushkin, like all his seniors and his peers, drew on the teaching experience and immense authority of Vaganova. But the greatest source of his pedagogic knowledge and skill was Ponomarev's classes, and so he was perceived at the school as a talented student of a brilliant master.

But by the early 1950s, Pushkin's methods were drawing more and more attention for a very obvious reason: the students who had been trained by him over several years of daily class were noticeably outstanding. They were distinguished by the thorough artistry with which they performed their variations and roles at graduation, a boldness and enviable mastery in complex dance passages, and a special sense of their own dignity (like their teacher's) that was free from affectation and from attempts to milk applause from the audience.

Then they began to speak of Pushkin in a different way—as a teacher who had raised the precepts of his predecessors to a new level. "Now teachers (and in particular Alexander Pushkin, a student of Ponomarev and in his day an excellent classical dancer) are rethinking and expanding this system," wrote Leonid Lavrovsky, chief choreographer of the Kirov and later of the Bolshoi, "because constant development is the living thing that is the school of Russian classical dance."[10]

What were the new features and elements in Pushkin's pedagogy, which he himself often stated was heavily dependent on Ponomarev's teaching? Let us try to compare Ponomarev's and Pushkin's classes.

First, the structure of the class.

"At the start of the class we did a difficult exercise at the barre, then two adagios in the center, which included turning and one or two jumps: he really liked giving us grand assemblé and grand jeté in attitude croisée and effacée, requiring noiseless landing." So Pushkin recalled his teacher's class at an evening devoted to Ponomarev. Pushkin is not quite accurate here, however. As has been mentioned, Ponomarev followed Vaganova in including three adagios in his class, as Pushkin recorded in his diaries in 1925. But Pushkin did it differently.

Let us compare the middle part of the exercise, which tells us a great deal about the class. Unfortunately, there is no record of the barre exercises in Ponomarev's class, which makes it impossible to juxtapose his class with Pushkin's, but the logic of the construction of these parts of the class is the same for all major teachers. Therefore, in comparing the center exercises we can obliquely compare the barre exercise as well.

Pushkin's exercises in the center were more developed than Vaganova's and Ponomarev's, even though he borrowed the principle of concentrated adagio from them. They consisted of two adagios, as well as combinations of battements fondus and grands battements jetés. And the last two combinations were, as in the adagio, replete with various kinds of turns. At the end of the center exercise before the allegro, Pushkin assigned a grande pirouette. This expansion of the center exercise was not accidental in the structure of Pushkin's class, but rather was the result of the turbulent growth of stage dancing, which he could not overlook. Therefore, in comparing the two graduation adagios, we must remember that the first comes from 1925 and is traditional in its number of steps and in a certain static element in the positions, while the second comes from 1966 and embodies pedagogical ideas that were sensitive to the needs of the times.

Thus, the adagio from Ponomarev's class (described in brief):

Feet in fifth position, right in front. Demi-plié, stretch the knees, développé à la seconde with the right (arms in second position), bring leg into effacée position (left arm in third, right in second position), tombée in fourth position, tours en dedans in first arabesque, end in demi-plié, fouetté à la seconde en dehors, demi-plié, fouetté à la seconde en dehors, demi-plié, pas de bourrée in fourth position, right leg in front, sixth port de bras, two tours à la seconde. End turn in à la seconde pose.

The adagio as a whole is rather simple for a graduating class (and of the three recorded by Pushkin, this is the most complex). What characteristic features here are important for the comparison?

First, the uniting of turns with développé, and second, the presence of a certain movement that could be termed basic—in this case, the position à la seconde.

Alexander Pushkin and Konstantin Sergeyev after examinations.

Natalya Dudinskaya and Alexander Pushkin after examinations.

It must also be noted that in Ponomarev's adagio there are jumps: in the third adagio, for instance, there are entrechats-six. The adagios almost always end with some kind of turn, and the final pose is the same as the one from which the turns are made.

Pushkin assigned two adagios in the center and additional combinations. The first adagio was done in conjunction with battements tendus and battements jetés; the second was based on various types of turns in poses. It is important to note that Pushkin introduced many turns into the other combinations of the exercise. Thus the end of the battements fondus combination was always built on turns in arabesque and attitude, and the grands battements jetés combination began with turns related to the original dance structure.

If we compare Pushkin's classes with those of Alexei Pisarev (also a student of Ponomarev's), we see that a large number of turns was an important trait in Pushkin's methodology. While Pisarev paid particular attention to the correct position of the feet in poses and assigned many développés—whence the static effect of his combinations—Pushkin demanded lightness in the poses and didn't like much "standing." Using many kinds of fouetté, he strove for unstrained muscle work. The poses took on a sharp clarity in his students, which is important in men's classical dance. Accelerated rhythm in his class affected the muscles (I am speaking of swift changes of combinations, not the tempo of the musical accompaniment), and tired students more, perhaps, but the volume of executed movement was greater than in Pisarev's class.

Naturally, Pisarev's pedagogical practice is edifying, too. Pushkin held Pisarev in great esteem and studied his methods closely. When Pisarev wrote a textbook on classical dance with V. S. Kostrovitskaya,[11] Pushkin remarked publicly, "I studied the manual thoroughly for a year and can confidently say that it will be of great assistance in choreography schools."[12] Pushkin followed the literature on classical dance very attentively. In analyzing the works of his colleagues, he formulated his own principles. "I think that there is no need to give detailed descriptions of classes, but simply to indicate which movement should be done when in the program,"[13] he commented in a discussion of *Primer of Classical Dance* by Nadezhda Bazarova and Varvara Mei.

Pushkin didn't approve of schematic lesson plans that constricted the teacher's ideas. He felt that the most important element in teaching was the logic behind composing a program. Here Pushkin shared the conviction of Vaganova, who wrote, "I cannot give a rigid plan for the construction of lessons. This is the realm where the decisive part is played by the experience and sensibility of the teacher."[14] This may be why Pushkin didn't write his own textbook on classical dance; he created marvelous combinations for teaching purposes, but he didn't consider it proper to impose them on others. Of course, there are sketches in his notes expressing his views on some issues in dance training (for instance, a description of the execution of all the forms of petit jeté, which he wrote about in 1961), but they never became an end in themselves. The notes make his position clear: movements have to be described in complex terms, including the work of the arms, head, and torso. He spoke of that approach in discussing the Bazarova–Mei textbook.

In choosing not to create textbooks, Pushkin was again like Ponomarev, who left no notes about his pedagogic methods.

But let us return to the comparison of Pushkin's adagio and Ponomarev's. Pushkin raised Ponomarev's class to a higher technical and dance level, while giving us an idea of Ponomarev's methods. The young Pushkin got his concentration on turns from his teacher and always considered them one of the most important aspects of men's

Alexander Pushkin, 1968.

classical dance. In his exercises, he stressed the variety of turns rather than static work on the academic forms of the adagio. And he was unequaled at joining them into combinations.

And so, on to Pushkin's "big" adagio in his graduating class of 1966.

Legs in fifth position, right in front. Arms open into second position. One tour with grand-plié in attitude croisée (left arm in third position, right in second), ending in effacée. Passé with left leg and développé in ecartée forward, after which the left leg lowers into fifth position behind and dégagé into first arabesque. Tour lent, demi-plié (right arm raised into third position), pas de bourrée in fifth position. Sissonne failli to the left and rise to half-toe on right leg in attitude croisée (left arm in third position, right in second), port de bras to the right then left (on half-toe), sixth form port de bras and two tours en dedans in attitude, ending in a pose effacée. Another demi-plié, pas de bourrée in fourth position and two tours en dedans in first arabesque. Pas failli in third arabesque on the right leg, jeté on the left in first arabesque, from which the leg is brought into position à la seconde, and fouetté en dehors through first position into a pose croisée in front with the right leg at 90 degrees with a finish in fifth position on half-toe (arms allongée).

This adagio was continued with a combination of battements tendus and battements jetés, which finished in tours en dehors and en dedans from second position. But this part does not interest us now, and we will not linger over it, even though it should be noted that Pushkin didn't write down a single similar continuation of the adagio from any of Ponomarev's classes. Apparently Ponomarev simplified some things in the examination class—for instance, he didn't assign battements tendus or battements jetés. Pushkin didn't follow this example; he assigned almost the entire range of the daily class for the examination, and he even extended the allegro. This was a question of principle: everything as usual, except for a slightly shortened exercise at the barre.

Do the adagios assigned by the two teachers have anything in common? Of course they do, and it can be formulated this way: The theme of the academic adagio was set by Ponomarev, and a variation on it on a higher technical and dance level was developed by Pushkin.

The principle of the two adagios' construction is similar: turns are the dominant note. There are many similar movements in both, for instance, the fouetté from the first arabesque into a pose à la seconde. Also, like Ponomarev, Pushkin introduced jumps into the adagio. But Ponomarev has only one instance of a jump in three adagios—the entrechat-six—while Pushkin included two jumps in one adagio: a sissonne failli and a jeté.

Yet while the increase in the number of jumps is a particular difference between Pushkin's adagio and Ponomarev's, the main difference between them is the different levels of technique and dancing ability required to perform them. Ponomarev's adagio, despite the turns, is rather static. Pushkin, by introducing the sissonne failli, pas failli, and jeté into the arabesque, expands the space in which the adagio is performed. He taught breadth in dancing, an important aspect of the adagio. It was aided by the port de bras in executing the grand plié as well as in the attitude and the half-toe position. The active participation of arm, torso, and head movements gave Pushkin's assigned adagios the appearance of dance miniatures.

This last point is significant. "Pushkin," recalled Mikhail Mikhailov, "preferred to assign learning combinations that contained an element of theater and thus helped his students fall in love with dance, feel an emotional uplift that led to artistry. In sum, besides the colossal practical benefit, these combinations gave the students great aesthetic pleasure."[15] Let us add that the pleasure was felt not only by

Pushkin's students but also—and perhaps even more so—by the uninvited audience that crowded in the doorways, drawn to the class.

It is important to note the great difference technically between Pushkin's adagio and Ponomarev's. In that sense, Ponomarev's adagio is only a sketch for Pushkin's painting. The extremely difficult tour from a grand plié in attitude, a transition after two tours in first arabesque into pas failli with a jeté to follow, a fouetté en dehors from pose à la second into a croisée forward, a rarely encountered form in classical dance—all these movements evince a very high technical level in the adagios assigned by Pushkin.

Basing the academic men's adagio on tradition, Pushkin perfected its structure. The two-part form of the "big" adagio took on a finished appearance. The first part consisted of battements développés, fouettés, port de bras, tours in big poses, and one or two jumps. The second part had types of battements tendus and battements jetés and various pirouettes en dehors and en dedans. The two parts were strictly separated, but the adagio nevertheless created an impression of an integrated whole, which was achieved by the introduction of port de bras into the second part of the adagio, too: battements tendus and battements jetés were performed with a transition of the arms from position to position. The development of dance ability was given serious attention even here.

Speaking of Pushkin's structure for the adagio, we must not fail to mention that at the choreographic school there was another point of view on this part of the men's class—for instance, the principles evidenced in Boris Shavrov's class. He had been a very famous premier dancer at the Kirov Theater, and he was an authoritative pedagogue who began teaching before Pushkin. Their manner of teaching differed, even though both instructors relied on the same foundation (Shavrov graduated from the school in the class of Victor Semenov, a strict classical dancer who retained the traditions of Legat's school in his pedagogy). Shavrov was extremely demanding in his observance of épaulement, watched closely for the position of the legs in poses croisée, effacée, ecartée, and insisted on emotional color in many movements. And his students were always excellently prepared physically and could bear heavy work loads easily. But his way of obtaining these results differed from Pushkin's. He usually assigned one adagio, constructed on various développés, fouettés, tours lents, and port de bras. And the port de bras was executed in poses with the leg raised at 90 degrees. A port de bras forward in the pose of first arabesque was his favorite passage. The second part of his adagio, like Pushkin's, consisted of battements tendus and battements jetés combinations. Shavrov's adagio was long—48 to 64 measures—and was repeated twice, from the right leg and then the left, which was the basis of the students' physical preparation. Pushkin developed stamina through intense pace, a greater number of jumps and various turns.

Pushkin's second adagio consisted almost completely of turns, which developed the students physically and technically. The tempo of this adagio increased and demanded dynamics in the execution of the steps. It included tours chaînés, pas chassé, fouetté en tournant executed in an accelerated tempo, which led to the next major combination—grands battements jetés.

The last combination before the allegro was the grande pirouette, which was always done twice: to the right and to the left. This was the rule for every class. Pushkin's students mastered turning in both directions thanks to all the combinations' being assigned on both legs. Neither lack of time nor the fatigue of the class (this would happen during the concert period) could alter that rule. "It's better to reduce the number of combinations, but we'll do everything from both legs," Alexander Ivanovich would say.

Pushkin was assiduous in maintaining creative discipline in class. He didn't permit jumps to be executed without the arms' being in proper position, and he forbade carelessness of form for the sake of increasing the number of turns. "You can't impress me with ten, I've seen sixteen pirouettes. Show me three done cleanly, stop in fifth position, and put your feet in demi-plié—and that will make me happy," he used to say with a chuckle to the "mechanical dancers."

Unfortunately, the new generation of teachers seems to forget this rule occasionally. They want to show off the high technical level of their students, overlooking the fact that classical dance is called classical precisely because it is about the perfection of line, smoothness of transition, and softness in landing after jumps. Ballet master Oleg Vinogradov once remarked about the "fruits" of the new methods: "Why do we almost never see any deeply developed roles or vivid characters in today's productions? Because the rehearsals where the basic work is supposed to be done are turned into lessons on dance technique. The coaches spend most of the time on teaching them how to do this or that step."[16] There is an element of casuistry in that statement. Choreographers can be as much to blame as the ballet artists for lack of "vivid characters" and "deeply developed roles." But there is no doubt that coaches are spending an inordinate amount of time on correcting defects in the dancers' preparation which should have been corrected in the classes of the ballet school. And they are required to teach not just how a step is made in principle, but how it should be executed correctly, according to the laws of classical dance. Too often, in the rush to acquire technique, dancers lose beauty and purity of execution.

Today, choreographers and ballet teachers are frequently called upon to pay attention to achievements in sports science, which is helping to improve

Above and opposite: During filming of the television program *Pushkin's Class*, 1968.

the performance of athletes. There are, of course, points of similarity in the development of the physical abilities of ballet artists and athletes (lightness and flexibility in gymnasts, using the entire potential of muscular energy in a minimal time in sprinters and jumpers). And the development of physical attributes does enhance a dancer's progress. But stamina and flexibility in a ballet artist do not guarantee correctness in executing dance steps. Even without going into the character and emotional aspects of ballet, let us try to define what we mean by the concept of classical "correctness," for it is here that the criteria lie for evaluating a dance teacher's work. If the students know how to perform all the movements of an exercise correctly, the teacher has taught successfully. If the students can do numerous pirouettes but don't have the professional skill to perform them cleanly, the teacher is not teaching them properly. This only seems to be a paradox. If the students have learned to jump and to spin dozens of pirouettes, then why should any sort of literacy be expected of them? But the point is that only with a literate and professional execution of the steps will the lines of the body in jumps and turns be harmonious, clean, and beautiful, and the shoulders not "creep up to the ears" during the turns. Time changes many things in art, but the basic laws for executing the movements of the classical exercise remain constant in ballet. And it is they that preserve the eternal beauty of classical dance.

    Pushkin created his combinations in a way that forced the student's body to move in relation to the inner laws of combining classical steps. Any ballet master, teacher, coach, or dancer given to improvisation can create an interesting combination of steps, but to create a combination that will contain a learning task that also fits into the whole structure of the class is a pedagogical talent. The steps must be combined so that performing them improperly will be uncomfortable for the students. Thus, if you turn your head in the direction of the glissade during a linking movement, it will not be in the right position when the leg moves for the fouetté in first arabesque, and this will make the body "shudder" in the air. "Learn how to free the leg that will be moving before the move, and changing the direction in which you're looking will help you execute the fouetté with coordination. In other words, don't exaggerate the turn of the head," Pushkin told his students. He was a real creator of such focused and edifying combinations. Pushkin, in fact, could have said nothing during class, simply demonstrating the order of the steps, and the learning process would have continued anyway. This was his natural teaching talent at its best. Its foundation was a complete mastery of classical dance, and he had a way of teaching its laws to each student in a thought-through and effective manner.

German Yanson wrote, "We often didn't notice the difficulties in learning certain movements because we were already prepared to perform them. When Pushkin assigned two pirouettes for the first time, we were already doing five or six, and instead of one turn in the air, we could do two or three. Learning was not a burden for us; on the contrary, it was a source of constant joy."[17] The planned program of his lessons allowed Pushkin to achieve marvelous results.

Let us return to the sports analogy. The best figure-skating coaches can get their skaters to learn complex technical elements in a short time. The explanation is simple: they break down the technically difficult elements into simple components and then, having worked on them thoroughly, bring the skater swiftly to a new technical level. This is the shortest and easiest path for the student, but a difficult one, demanding vast experience and sensitivity in the instructor. Knowing how to break down complex movements into component parts and preparing the student physically and psychologically to combine the simple elements, to identify the moment when he is prepared to execute the entire combination, that is teaching talent.

And this is the path Pushkin took, as can be seen from the combinations he assigned in the lower classes.

In the adagio for the fifth class (we do not know when it was created, but we can assume it dates to the late 1940s), we can find the basis of the complex elements that will be embodied in the combinations of Pushkin's graduating class.

Fifth position, right leg in front. Grand plié followed by going on half-toe. Développé front with right leg on croisée (right arm in third position, left in second). Passé with the right leg (head to the left, arms in first position) and transition to first arabesque. Tour lent on demi-plié, up onto half-toe in attitude effacée, allongée, pas de bourrée in fourth position, preparation and transition to pose à la seconde. Tour lent en dedans to pose écartée to the back, left leg lowers into fifth position in the back. Sissonne fermée in third arabesque, sissonne fermée in second arabesque, left leg is lowered to fifth position in front. Pas chassé forward to effacée, tombée, pas de bourrée in fourth position. And in conclusion, one tour en dehors.

Technically the adagio is simple enough, but it contains preparation for turns in à la seconde and attitude. There are also two jumps, at first simple sissonne fermée, but in the second jump there is a leg change, which prepares the student for the more complex sissonne failli. Finally, the pas chassé trains the students to move around the floor during the adagio, which will be practiced in a more complicated way in the senior classes. In other words, Pushkin's entire complex of demands in regard to the adagio finds a simple embodiment in this combination. And this holds for all parts of his class.

Therefore, it is no surprise that Pushkin's students mastered the "text" of any classical variation with enviable ease once they were onstage. Their mastery was based not

The class for soloists. In foreground: Alexander Pushkin, Vadim Budarin, Sergei Vikulov.

only on the number of movements they had learned but also on the quality of their mastery of those movements.

Pushkin's classes revealed the profound treasures of classical dance. The road to those treasures began with exercises at the barre, which lay the groundwork for a ballet artist. The signature of a Pushkin student was developed from the first plié at the barre. So let us return to the start of the class, which we skipped earlier in order to examine the new developments in the center exercises.

A characteristic of the barre exercises in the senior classes was that all the movements were assigned in combination with forms of fouetté and turns. Only the first two combinations, pliés and battements tendus (which were always combined with battements jetés in Pushkin's class), were given without additional complications. These combinations warmed up the muscles and communicated precision to the body, for even the first pliés were performed with simple port de bras on half-toe, which didn't allow the arms and torso to relax.

Interestingly, in the fifth class in the late 1940s (an adagio from this class was given above), Pushkin assigned pliés without port de bras; the battements tendus were usually combined with battements jetés, but in the third spot he has battements fondus rather than the ronds de jambe par terre that he used in the classes of the 1960s. This is no accident. In a comparable class noted in Vaganova's book *Basic Principles of Classical Ballet*, it is battement fondu combined with battement frappée that is in the third spot.[18] Vaganova's influence on her contemporaries was enormous, and naturally, Pushkin didn't escape it. She allowed the combination of battement fondu with battement frappé and of rond de jambe par terre with rond de jambe en l'air. When she introduced these blends, the battement fondu was moved from the fourth spot in the exercise to the third, and the rond de jambe par terre to the fourth. The structure of the exercise changed. The muscles were prepared in a different way for work in the center: the move of the battement fondu to third place—that is, ahead—made it a bit harder on the muscles. This is because the grand plié, battement fondu, and battement développé all develop strength rather than lightness in the muscle. For male dancing, a lightness in the leg while executing large jumps is very important, which is why, later on, Pushkin gave up Vaganova's order of movements, which were more appropriate for the women's class than the men's. He put the rond de jambe par terre in third place in the exercise combined with the grand rond de jambe, which develops lightness.

It is important to mention the following. Comparing later classes with the class of the late 1940s lets us answer the question: Did the structure of Pushkin's class remain unchanged throughout his thirty-eight-year teaching career? Students who worked with him in the last fifteen years maintain that his class didn't change structurally. Every lesson brought many interesting, unexpected combinations, but each movement had its assigned place and there were no changes in that sense. But this does not apply to his entire career. The exercises of the 1940s differ from those of the 1960s in the order of movements. I have already mentioned the place of the battement fondu. We see that in the late period of his teaching, Pushkin tried to unite the sharp battements frappés with petits battements sur le cou-de-pied, which he placed before the final grands battements jetés. Here it does not matter that we are comparing the exercises of the middle and senior classes, because in his notes on the exercises for the sixth class during his early years of teaching (for a class that on the technical level might be seventh grade) we find the same structure as in the exercises for the fifth class.

We can presume that the structure of the exercise took shape in its final form during the mid-1950s, when the principles of Pushkin's method had matured and

Alexander Pushkin in a class
at the Choreographic School.

become independent. His growth as a teacher was particularly noticed in those years at the school. In the teachers' council meeting on February 15, 1956, N. P. Ivanovsky, the artistic director of the school, stated: "In 1950, Kamkova, Shiripina and Pushkin taught the fifth and sixth classes. Now they are the teachers of the leading senior classes."[19] A year later, after Pushkin's report on his work with the new and exceptionally difficult class of students from Kazakhstan, Ivanovsky once again spoke of Pushkin's achievements: "I believe that the students of the Kazakh group are in reliable hands, thanks to which miracles were performed in a very short time—just five months."[20]

In Pushkin's structure for the exercise at the barre, the number of steps within a combination grew over the years, which is a reflection of the development of ballet art in general. The increase in the work load in ballets of the early 1960s did not go unnoticed by the teacher. He had to prepare dancers to perform in new complex works like *Legend of Love* by Yuri Grigorovich and *Leningrad Symphony* by Igor Belsky. The class also polished the quality of line so essential to the dances of Ferkhad; they practiced with the Fisherman's flight from *Coast of Hope*. Note that in the exercise at the barre in 1967, five of the eight combinations ended in fixed points—in attitude, effacée, croisée, and écartée. In the interior monologues of *Legend of Love*, the dancer needed full mastery of movements that were unusual in male dancing—battement développés, tours lents, and port de bras in the large poses. The exercise at the barre that focused on executing large poses, tours lents, and fouettés helped the future artist master the new works of the late 1950s–early 1960s.

Pushkin regarded the exercise at the barre as the first step toward dancing on the stage. Of course, Cecchetti too prepared dancers with his exercise at the barre for explosive jumps and sharp moves. His workout consisted of nine movements, six of which were directed at developing speed in the muscles. The structure of the exercise developed the ability to move the legs sharply in jumps. After the first pliés, Cecchetti assigned grands battements jetés, and then battements tendus, and so on. Pushkin didn't introduce such radical changes, but while respecting the basic values of the Russian school of teaching classical dance, he followed stage practice very closely and made corrections in his class to accommodate new choreography.

The exercises at the barre and in the center prepared the students for the main part of the class. For Pushkin it was the allegro. From the first assemblés to the last pirouettes or tours en l'air in variations and codas, Pushkin developed the sharpness of the beats, airiness and strength in jumps, softness in landing, flawlessness in pose in the air and in the final stop. And he demanded that all this be achieved in a restrained manner, with a steady sense of épaulement, which is basic to the culture of dance. Vaganova used to say that you can recognize the school by the port de bras. Pushkin's students could be recognized by the manner of their jumps, as well. "Lighter, calmer. No effort. Spring in the glissade, so that the push-off is almost without any force," Pushkin would say, conveying his own precision to the student.

The allegro began with small assemblé, échappé, jeté, sissone fermée in various poses. Pushkin liked to introduce brisé with a finish in fifth position and brisé dessu-dessou into the second jump combination. These steps are rarely found in the start of the allegro with other teachers; they are usually placed at the very end, so that the leg muscles will start working impulsively and sharply after the big jumps. They are also done last because executing the brisé forms requires very well warmed-up muscles. Pushkin would also assign two combinations of sharp beats, most frequently entrechat quatre, royal, entrechat-six, échappé battu—that is, beats that do not require progression but are aimed only at developing lightness and clarity of the legs.

Pushkin's order of steps had its raison d'être. In principle, the brisé resembles petit jeté battu. But the latter ends on one foot and the brisé on two, which is much easier to do in the first combination of the allegro. Pushkin managed to warm up the muscles with his exercises at the barre and in the center, and he felt that after the assemblé and échappé his students were ready to execute brisé, which is why he gave it before the petit jeté. Of course, brisé dessu-dessou only begins with both legs, in fifth position, and then is performed with the push-off of one leg and the kick of the other with cou-de-pied at 45 degrees, and ends on one leg. But even this form of brisé has its analogy in jeté. That is the "jeté to the side without poses," as Pushkin called it. We've already mentioned that Pushkin once wrote down his opinions of the principles of executing petits jetés, which he divided into three types: the first and second are executed en face, the third in poses and épaulement. Petits jetés develop the ability to turn, the strength of push-off from one leg, the ability to coordinate movements of legs, head, and arms. Brisé in fifth position and brisé dessu-dessou are analogous in what they teach, and so Pushkin placed them in the beginning of the allegro, without violating the logic of the lesson's structure set by the founders of the Russian school of teaching dance. Thus, in basing himself on the experience of his predecessors while taking his own experience into account, he perfected the beginning of the allegro. As always, Pushkin was not afraid of innovation and was receptive to everything that seemed reasonable.

The transcript of the methodology meeting of the teachers of classical dance at the Leningrad Choreographic School on October 16, 1959, indicates that this meeting reexamined the curriculum of the experimental six-year course that had been instituted in Vaganova's lifetime with her direct involvement. Her authority at the school seemed inviolate, yet Pushkin argued persuasively, indicating the strengths and the weaknesses of the program. Some teachers wanted to simplify the program by reducing the battement tendu pour batteries in the first experimental class. Pushkin disagreed: "This movement must be kept, for it's especially beneficial for the boys." He systematically assigned that movement in the exercise at the barre, which is why his students could do beats so brilliantly. But then Pushkin accepted a series of reductions, explaining it this way: "After all, we intended this program for the best students of the experimental class. But unfortunately, there aren't any."[21] Expediency took precedence in his mind.

In creating jump combinations, Pushkin was concerned with training students in both the broad and the light dancing that are characteristic of the Russian school. We have already noted that even in the adagio he accustomed the students to conquer a great deal of stage space and to move with ease and grace. In a lesson for the fifth class, in the allegro, there is this sequence of steps: Fifth position, right leg in front. Sissonne tombée forward into croisée, pas chassé, assemblé with left to the back, grand changement de pieds.[22] This is an extremely simple combination, consisting of four movements, organically intertwined, but it serves so many purposes. First, the two beginning movements are preparation for a complex sissonne en tournant en l'air while traveling on the diagonal. Second, the combination trains the torso to move. Third, it teaches the student to cover space during dance. The technical level of the movements is not high, but as a whole they function as an excellent teaching aid.

Let us compare this combination with another that Pushkin assigned to the graduating class. In the structure of the allegro of the two classes, the combinations hold almost the same place (one is fourth, the other, third).

Fifth position, right foot in front. Sissonne tombée in first arabesque, cabriole in this pose, pas failli, coupé with right behind left, and assemblé to the front with the left. It is all performed to the left. Preparation in third arabesque on right leg and grand fouetté in attitude effacée, then tombée on right leg toward point 2 (on the diagram of the studio on p. 64) and cabriole in pose of first arabesque. For the finish, pas failli and temps levé in pose attitude croisée on left leg (arms in third position).

This combination, like the preceding one, includes a sissonne tombée, but the sequence is changed. In the first combination, the sissonne was followed by a simple pas chassé, while in the second, a much more technically difficult cabriole in pose first arabesque follows. In the first combination there is a simple assemblé after the pas chassé, while in the second the assemblé is performed in sequence with a pas coupé. The change of leg occurs in the first combination in the grand changement de pieds, and in the second through a complex sequence of movements: pas failli, pas coupé, assemblé. An increase in technical difficulty is noticeable throughout, but the logic of the steps' structure is the same. The combinations include the same steps (for instance, sissonne tombée) and both are directed at developing mobility and lightness. We can see that the first combination is excellent preparation for the second.

In analyzing the laws of mixing steps within each combination, we see what governed Pushkin's decisions on sequences. Understanding the logic of his combinations means determining what is most important in the principles of construction and therefore in the performance of classical dance.

The first thing that everyone who ever studied in Pushkin's class remembers is the constant feeling of joy. Executing his combinations was an actual pleasure. It was all so organic, so extraordinarily gracefully put together, that it was a pleasure to be dancing—and I mean dancing, not simply working on mastering sequences of steps.

Glissade, cabriole fermée to the side, sissonne tombée, again cabriole, but now in first arabesque, then pas failli, coupé, assemblé croisée (arms in third position), rise to half-toe in fifth position. Plié, sissonne tombée on effacée left leg, sissonne in first arabesque, pas chassé along the diagonal up, cabriole fouetté in fourth arabesque, Cessna tombée to the right (like the first time), pas chassé and sissonne à la seconde with a turn fouetté in a jump. End in first arabesque in plié.

An amazing combination, a small masterpiece of Pushkin's choreographic imagination. A flawless situation of steps in space. Graphically, the composition can be depicted in the following way:

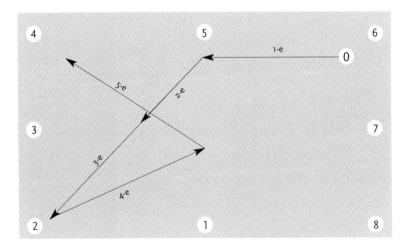

0 is starting position.
Arrows indicate direction of movement.

The direction of the movement of the three forms of connecting steps (glissade, pas failli, sissonne tombée) changes four times. Three different types of cabriole are united in one combination. The difficult cabriole fermée in écartée is replaced by the simpler one in first arabesque, and the third is the most complex—cabriole fouetté en tournant in pose fourth arabesque. There is a logic in the introduction of the cabriole: the complex virtuoso steps alternate with simpler ones. The combination is not overwhelmed with difficulties—there is a logical progression from difficult to simple and vice versa. Pushkin used this three-part form for men's variations as the foundation of his combinations for medium and big jumps. The men's variations in the ballets of the great Petipa generally use big jumps in the first part, turns in the second, and virtuoso turns in the air or big jumps, like those in the first, in the third part. Pushkin's combinations were miniature forms of such variations. This reflected his view on the need to prepare dancers to master the peak of classical dance—the variations. This naturally brings to mind Vaganova, who maintained that the adagio was not sufficient to show a dancer's mettle (since the ballerina is helped by her partner's support). "But to come out on the stage and make an impression in a variation is something else: here is where the subtleties and finish of your dance will be shown."[23] She would tell her students over and over: "Now show what you can do in the variation!"

Contemporary Russian ballet pedagogy has other approaches for training ballet artists. Asaf Messerer, in the past a famous Bolshoi Theater dancer, individualistic ballet master, and authoritative teacher who devoted half a century to teaching, developed a methodology that differs significantly from Pushkin's principles. Of course, we must bear in mind that Messerer's class is intended for soloists of the Bolshoi and not for students, which naturally colors his aims. Pushkin taught both at the theater and at the school.

The principle of structuring a class at the theater remained the same as for a class at the school, but with reduced combinations. However, Messerer also based his methods on the work of V. D. Tikhomirov, who had taught for many years at both the Bolshoi school and theater. Tikhomirov introduced the so-called method of a single step. "Following the pedagogical principles of Vasily Tikhomirov," Messerer wrote, "I developed individual choreographic themes during each weekly course of lessons."[24]

Tikhomirov's "method of a single step" sprang from the influence of the Italian school, which had a program of classes involving a weekly cycle. Tikhomirov, sent to St. Petersburg after graduation from the Moscow Theater School, learned about Cecchetti's classes and grew interested in his subsequent work. Tikhomirov's single-step method harkens back to Cecchetti's school; the entire class is built on combinations of various forms and types of a single movement. Each Tikhomirov class had a dominant theme that was the basis for all the combinations. In an anthology of tributes to him,[25] there is an example of an allegro from such a class. The dominant feature of the allegro is the cabriole. Pushkin once proposed a combination that put together almost all forms of the cabriole encountered in Tikhomirov's five combinations in the allegro, and this was without the specific aim of devoting the class to the cabriole alone. But in subsequent combinations he assigned other forms of the step which were not in Tikhomirov's combinations. And there were many other jumps in the allegro as well.

Pushkin always covered many classical steps in just one class. They were varied deftly, and not a single one failed to receive due attention. Messerer, as an experienced and thoughtful master, even as a follower of Tikhomirov, had to take into account the qualities of the St. Petersburg principles of instruction, the significance of which he always stressed. But he did say that "Each class must have its special purpose, theme, problem, or leitmotif."[26] This single focus can, however, lead to an impoverishment of teaching in classical dance, especially if the teacher is not endowed with a unique ability to endlessly vary a single step. In his classes, Messerer himself often acted more as a ballet master than a teacher. Original mixtures and connections, sharp changes in direction of movements, despite their lack of variety, are the signature of Messerer the teacher. His classes tend to be concert-like rather than class-like, despite their declared intention of deepening the mastery of a step. There is good reason why he staged *Ballet Class* at the Bolshoi. But for Pushkin, a class was not a "gala performance." His original combinations, which were often stunning, were created for solid training and educational purposes.

Incidentally, the dislike of flash and pomp was evident in the examinations for Pushkin's class. He didn't allow the examination to turn into a recital. Even if he had an exceptionally strong student in the class, Pushkin didn't distinguish him with special combinations; on the contrary, he kept him in the general group, showing that he taught everyone the same way, that they all had the same preparation, and that this one dances better because of his attributes and talent. For that same reason, at the examination class almost all the graduates danced fragments of variations or codas from the ballets of the classic legacy. Pushkin particularly liked Siegfried's coda from Act II of *Swan Lake*—he liked it for the breadth of its first jeté, followed by the entrelacé with beats and the precision of the ending of the tours en l'air in first arabesque. He often assigned it for the graduation examination.

His rehearsals were a natural extension of Pushkin's classes, bringing young performers into productions of the current repertory or into school productions to be shown on the theater's stage. When the Kirov Theater went on tour, Pushkin's students were replacement dancers, often in leading roles. They quickly caught the style and character of adagios and variations, for many were familiar from class, where they learned the laws of performance mastery, indispensable on the stage.

Filling in often requires learning a part in a short time. I had to pass that test myself. I was given twenty days to prepare the role of the Youth in Fokine's *Chopiniana*. Our class work came in handy then, for we had all danced fragments from the ballet's different variations and codas. Every day, before class was over, we went over a part of the lyrical variation of the Youth, so unexpectedly explosive and abrupt in its second part. Pushkin gave us a complete understanding of the change of épaulement, port de bras. Watching his ideal version made it easier to grasp the style of the variation—the most difficult in this ballet. "Bring the legs deeper in the entrechat-six. We've already done that today, and we repeated the battement pour batteries twice, especially for you." Those words could have been heard in Pushkin's class in May 1968. A few years passed. And in a different theater, when a guardian of the classics in the "periphery" of the country, bearing the collection of "his" ballets from one stage to another, started to demonstrate the Youth's variation, his body took command. The mazurka sounded and the arms, legs, head, and torso "remembered" what his teacher had shown him long ago. "Organically! Not bad. Let's try this version." And so Pushkin went on teaching. Invisibly, he entered ballet studios where his foot had never trod.

The daily class for theater soloists didn't include executing variations, but thinking back on how the classes ended, my memory serves up the finale of the variation of the Genius of the Ocean from the old *Little Hump-backed Horse*, or the coda from *Swan Lake*, or the middle section of the Prince's variations from *The Sleeping Beauty*. It was Yuri Soloviev who performed the variation of the Genius of the Ocean incomparably. Without apparent effort he did

The class for soloists. Left to right: Yuri Soloviev, Mikhail Baryshnikov, Vadim Desnitsky, Alexander Manoshkin.

the double tours en l'air three times, to the delight and awe of onlookers. Soloviev had an affinity for Pushkin's manner of teaching, even though he had graduated from Boris Shavrov's class. Calmly, in the Pushkin way, without excess emotion, he brilliantly performed all the combinations. At the end of class, if he had a performance in the offing, Soloviev would do some of his variations: Pushkin's accompanist, Serafim Bodunov, who worked with him in the latter years, knew the entire ballet repertoire and played whatever the soloist requested. It wasn't mandatory, but it was a kind of tradition. "Alexander Ivanovich, take a look!" The teacher was always happy to prompt a forgotten detail or correct an inaccuracy.

He always helped everyone. If necessary, he staged numbers for his students: classical duets and waltzes. He didn't have a purely choreographic gift and didn't attempt full-blown compositions, but his sketches revealed not only exquisite professional knowledge but a lively feel for dance, for organic sequences of classical steps. His staging of Massenet's "Adagio" conveyed the dancers' relationship through technically uncomplicated air lifts, but the promenades were unique, finishing harmoniously with tours en dehors either from pose à la seconde or from fourth position. By the way, Pushkin never boasted to his students about his mastery as a ballet partner, even though they knew that in his day he had handled this responsibility very well. His repertoire included the role of Asak in *The Ice Maiden*, where the virtuosity of the duets seemed to stretch the limits of the possible. "In his confident, knowing hands, a ballerina never had to worry about a complicated maneuver," Mikhail Mikhailov recounted. "Whether she was turning, invisibly spun in incredible turns on the floorboards, or held somewhere above his head, she could feel totally calm."[27] All of Pushkin's remarks on the difficulties of duet dancing were extremely concrete and precise. He was brilliant in his partnering class, and indeed, the foundation of his teaching

Alexander Pushkin at home.

career was this discipline. Even when he had his own class, he continued teaching duet dancing until the very end of the 1950s. In the 1958–59 school year, it happened that the teachers of the partnering class at the school were all leading soloists in the theater and had all been sent abroad on tour, one after the other. Out of necessity Pushkin substituted for them all, carrying on the school's instruction.

Selflessness! Pushkin's entire life embodied that concept. Every day for a half century he entered the ballet studio. Every morning Alexander Pushkin could be seen there, first as a student, then as an artist, and, finally, as a teacher. He left the studio exhausted yet happy. The day had been spent on what he loved. The days of his life were varied: some joyous, others sad, a few profoundly dramatic. But essentially he was profoundly happy at having tied his fate forever to his beloved ballet.

He earned an illustrious place in the history of ballet teaching. Not given to theorizing, not having written any books, he left behind a memory first of all in the generation of dancers whom he taught so brilliantly and who are devoted to the art of the ballet, the best of whom are the pride of modern ballet. The universal fame of Rudolf Nureyev and Mikhail Baryshnikov, worthy of their teacher, promoted his recognition worldwide.

With a strong sense of the continuity of time (which is characteristic of ballet in general), Pushkin organically used the experience of his predecessors, the practices of the Italian and French schools and of the Russian school based on them. At first intuitively and then consciously and eventually with great focus, he gathered up everything accumulated by the teachers of the past. He cherished in his memory and gave to his own students what he had learned from his mentors, Vladimir Ponomarev and Agrippina Vaganova. But every one of his classes was a step forward, a search for more perfect paths for raising young dancers.

Ponomarev's class could be described as intelligent, academically strict, and calm (containing the wisdom of history), while Pushkin the teacher listened more closely to the pulse of contemporary art, followed its development sensitively, and without damaging the foundation built new "floors" of the choreographic school. In this he was closer to Vaganova, who felt that teaching methods had to undergo constant change without losing touch with the great past, and who wrote: "I personally am constantly introducing new steps, new movements that prepare the artists in the class of perfection and the young women in school to work in accordance with planned productions."[28] Pushkin didn't structure his class program in accordance with planned productions, but one could always feel the heartbeat of the theater in his class. He watched the attempts to find new elements in choreography and he enriched his class with them. The synthesis of the Russian classical school with the achievements of his contemporaries was embodied both in his daily classes at the school and at the theater.

Today there is much discussion about the structure of class at the theater and in the school. There are teachers who feel that classes have to be built on a single foundation in both school and theater, with the most important focus being the development of the physical, technical, and dancing abilities of students and artists. Another point of view holds that school (the senior classes) is a training ground for professionalism, for training a dancer and his technique, while the class at the theater is merely for supporting the soloist's physical form, since rehearsals develop artistry and technique.

Pushkin was a fervent adherent of the former point of view. In school classes and in the classes for soloists of the theater, he synthesized the principles of education and artistic training. His class strengthened his students physically, promoted the development of their technique, and taught people not to work but to dance. He demanded

Alexander Pushkin, in one of the last photographs taken of him.

The grave of Alexander Pushkin and Xenia Yurgenson at the Bolsheokhtinsky Cemetery, St. Petersburg.

that everything be done with thought, first by getting to the heart of every movement and the inner structure of any combination. It is no wonder that so many of his charges became teachers.

We often say "Students of Pushkin." It would be more accurate to say "Students of the Pushkin school." But even there we do not get to the essence. His class was not a compendium of schematic combinations that can be presented for exact repetition. Pushkin's class was a historically formed and logically based pedagogical principle embodied in assigned combinations that contained enormous teaching potential and, at the same time, artistic potential. His natural talent for creating combinations grew over the years into an incomparable mastery that remains legendary for all who attended his class.

Pushkin's death was a terrible blow for all his students. There are losses that change a way of life and make one regard everything differently. With the loss of our teacher, many of us, his charges and disciples, felt a void and a sense of professional vulnerability. With whom could we check our dancing, to whom could we turn for advice and support, who would always be with us, selflessly, both in the rehearsal studio and in life?

I can imagine what Baryshnikov was feeling as he smashed his hands blindly at the wall, the door, the glass of the lobby of Pushkin's house when he learned of his teacher's death.

The terrible news reached me far from Architect Rossi Street. March 21, 1970, was the premiere of *Don Quixote* in the Saratov Theater. I was dancing Basil. During the third act, just before the final pas de deux, I was handed a telegram. They thought it was one of congratulations from Leningrad. How can you dance after receiving news like that? But I had to dance, and dance the way Alexander Ivanovich had taught me to. I remembered the graduation concert at the Kirov Theater, when the agitated, weary Pushkin sat in the dressing room and said softly to me, "Good for you. You conquered yourself. The death of a father is terrible. But our life is here, and we can never give up." It was only ten years later that I read these lines in Pushkin's diary: "A half hour late. I returned from the theater, and Father was dead. How can I go on…." I realized then that Pushkin hadn't been consoling me, hadn't been teaching me; he had led me through the milestones of his own life, sharing the experiences he had suffered. He made me wiser with that experience and prepared me for the torment of the premiere in 1970. To go out on the stage at that moment meant living up to his commandment.

The thread was not broken. His students continue the teacher's precepts.

Soon after Pushkin's death, a tradition was born at the Maryinsky Theater: on the anniversary of his death, the class of soloists performs his class.

Over the last years, dancers from other ballet schools have joined the theater, and new generations have grown up on Architect Rossi Street. But many of the newcomers join Pushkin's students at the barre. Vladlen Semyonov, in a quiet, calm voice that somehow resembles Alexander Ivanovich's intonations, assigns the first combination: "Pliés, battement tendus with jetés." And then it's the adagio in the center. It's all so achingly familiar, but some things are gone, lost to memory. "Pas ciseaux ending in first arabesque. Don't hop. Deepen the demi-plié." And again: "Assemblé, entrechat-quatre, assemblé…."

A lovely tradition. It will live on, I believe, until the very last of Alexander Ivanovich's students ends his career. We are giving a talented man and teacher his due. New links connecting the past with the future.

And I remember ... the compact, thin man of medium height walking unhurriedly down the corridors of the school on Architect Rossi Street—the street that used to be called Theater Street and which, in the words of Tamara Karsavina, "remained a consecrated ground of daily work, a link in the chain of continuity. A nursery of creative search, a haven of repair."[29]

The class in memory of Alexander Pushkin, March 20, 1973. Left to right: Victor Semenov, Valentin Kozlovsky (accompanist), Alexander Chistyakov, Andrei Bosov, Sergei Berezhnoi, Alexander Manoshkin, Mikhail Baryshnikov, V. Bondarenko, Nikolai Kovmir, V. Ivantsov, Sergei Fedyanin, Redjep Abdyev, Vadim Desnitsky, Georgy Dzevulsky, Alexander Pavlovsky.

Notes

CHAPTER 1

1   TsGALI [Central State Literary Archives], St. Petersburg, f. 4462, op. 3, art. 481.

2   Archive of the A. Ia. Vaganova A. R. B. [Agrippina Yakovlevna Vaganova Choreographic School].

3   Personal archive of A. I. Pushkin. Diary. These diaries, kept by Pushkin between 1919 and 1947, will be cited throughout.

4   Transcript of board meeting of the State Academic Theater School. TsGALI, St. Petersburg, f. 4462, op. 1, art. 108, p. 3.

5   Iu. Brodersen, "*La Source* (at the Ballet School)," *Rabochii i teatr* [Worker and the Theater], No. 16 (1925): 20.

6   S. R., "On the Graduation Production at the Academic Ballet School," *Krasnaia panorama* [Red Panorama], No. 17 (1925): 16.

7   S. Abashidze, "Ballet Academy," *Krasnaia panorama*, No. 17 (1925): 15.

8   Iu. Brodersen, "Don't Get Stuck in Stereotyped Forms!" *Rabochii i teatr*, No. 17 (1925): 21.

9   Ch. Tim, "The World and Art" (clipping). A. I. Pushkin archive.

10   S. R., "On the Graduation Production at the Academic Ballet School," p. 16.

11   Abashidze, "Ballet Academy," p. 15.

12   V. Iving, "Studio of Dramatic Ballet. 'Exploits of the Three,' " *Zhizn' iskusstva* [Life of Art], No. 20 (1925): 10.

13   Iu. Brodersen, "Academic Ballet School," *Rabochii i teatr*, No. 9 (1924): 20.

14   S. Mokulskii, " 'The Red Poppy' in Leningrad," *Zhizn' iskusstva*, No. 5 (1929): 10–11.

15   Conversation with N. P. Bazarova, March 16, 1974.

16   See A. Aleksandrovich, "What Is to Be Done with Ballet?" *Zhizn' iskusstva*, No. 5 (1925): 8.

17   See "On Ballet Reform," *Zhizn' iskusstva*, No. 26 (1928).

18   A. Gvozdev, " 'The Ice Maiden' (the Staging in Gatoba)," *Zhizn' iskusstva*, No. 18 (1927): 5.

19 I. Sollertinskii, " 'The Nutcracker' at the Leningrad State Ballet," *Zhizn' iskusstva*, No. 44 (1929): 5.

20 Ibid.

21 Quoted in K. Armashevskaia and I. Vainonen, *Baletmeister Vainonen* [Ballet Master Vainonen] (Moscow, 1971), p. 77.

22 A. Gvozdev, "The Flames of Paris," *Rabochii i teatr*, No. 32–33 (1932): 4–5.

23 E. Gershuni, "Actors in Ballet," *Rabochii i teatr*, No. 34 (1932): 8–9.

24 Conversation with K. I. Yurgenson, October 17, 1972.

25 L. Blok, "Laurencia," *Iskusstvo i zhizn'* [Art and Life], No. 5 (1939): 36–37.

26 A. Movshenson, "Graduation Performance of the Choreographic School," *Za sovetskoe iskusstvo* [For Soviet Art], No. 113 (1947): 4.

27 I. Venert, "Second Birth," *Za sovetskoe iskusstvo*, No. 1 (1946): 4.

28 S. Rozenfel'd, "Renaissance of Men's Dance," *Iskusstvo i zhizn'*, No. 6 (1940): 8–9.

CHAPTER 2

1 From A. I. Pushkin's speech at the meeting in honor of the seventy-fifth birthday of V. I. Ponomarev at the Leningrad Choreographic School. A. I. Pushkin archive.

2 Transcript of the meeting of ballet teachers at the St. Petersburg Theater School. TsGIA, St. Petersburg, f. 198, art. 4618.

3 A. Volynskii, *Kniga likovanii* (Leningrad, 1925), p. 164. Trans. in part by Seymour Barofsky as *The Book of Exultation*, in *Dance Scope* (Spring 1971): 16–35 and (Fall/Winter 1971–72): 43–53.

4 Quoted in Cyril W. Beaumont and Stanislas Idzikowski, *A Manual of the Theory and Practice of Classical Theatrical Dancing (Méthode Cecchetti)* (London, 1922; repr. New York, 1975), p. 21.

5 Tamara Karsavina, *Teatral'naia ulitsa*. 1930. Trans. as *Theatre Street: The Reminiscences of Tamara Karsavina* (London, 1981), p. 111.

6 M. M. Fokine, *Protiv techeniia* [Against the Current] (Leningrad and Moscow, 1962), p. 108.

7 Ibid., p. 148.

8 Ibid., p. 102.

9 E. M. Liukom, *Moia rabota v balete* [My Work in the Ballet] (Leningrad, 1940), No. 5.

10 Nicolas Legat, *The Story of the Russian School*. Trans. by Sir Paul Dukes (London, 1932), p. 17.

11 Ibid., p. 20.

12 Fokine, *Protiv techeniia*, p. 108.

13 Fedor Lopukhov, *Shest'desiat let v balete* [Sixty Years in Ballet] (Moscow, 1966), p. 83.

14 Ibid., p. 84.

15 Ibid.

16 Legat, *The Story of the Russian School*, p. 70.

17 L. D. Blok, *Klassicheskii tanets* [Classical Dance] (Moscow, 1987), p. 336.

18 Ibid.

19 Fedor Lopukhov, *Khoreograficheskie otkrovennosti* [Choreographic Frankness] (Moscow, 1972), p. 170.

20 See Legat, *The Story of the Russian School*, p. 72.

21 Blok, *Klassicheskii tanets*, p. 336.

22 Legat, *The Story of the Russian School*, p. 15.

23 Ibid., p. 31.

24 V. Krasovskaia, *Russkii baletnyi teatr nachala XX veka. I. Khoreografy* [Russian Ballet Theater of the Early Twentieth Century. I. Choreographers] (Leningrad, 1971), p. 106.

25 M. Mikhailov, *Zhizn' v balete* [Life in Ballet] (Moscow and Leningrad, 1966), p. 195.

26 Lopukhov, *Shest'desiat let v balete*, p. 200.

27 Conversation with A. V. Ponomareva on February 14, 1976.

28 A. Messerer, *Tanets. Mysl'. Vremia* [Dance. Thought. Time] (Moscow, 1979), p. 17.

29 Quoted in P. Gusev, "Muzhestvennyi talant" [Courageous Talent]. In: A. Ermolaev, *Sbornik statei* [Collection of Articles] (Moscow, 1974), p. 64.

30 M. Churova, "Vsegda i vo vsem v poiske" [Seeking Always and in Everything]. In: Ermolaev, *Sbornik statei*, p. 135.

31 Iu. Slonimskii, "Operezhaia vremia" [Overtaking Time]. In: Ermolaev, *Sbornik statei*, p. 10.

32 Ibid.

33 See "Controversial Questions in Ballet Theater," *Iskusstvo i zhizn'*, No. 4 (1939): 24–25.

CHAPTER 3

1 Conversation with N. I. Kovmir on April 5, 1974.

2 Conversation with N. P. Bazarova on March 16, 1974.

3 *Dance and Dancers*, September 1966, p. 13.

4 Letter from V. Veselovskii dated December 27, 1962. A. I. Pushkin personal archive.

5 Letter from E. Bischoff dated October 16, 1961. A. I. Pushkin personal archive.

6 Letter from G. Barbu dated May 3, 1955. A. I. Pushkin personal archive.

7 N. A. Dobroliubov, *Sobr. Soch v 3-x t.* [Collected Works in 3 vols.], vol. 3 (Moscow, 1952), p. 247.

8 Letter from L. V. Oshurko to the author dated December 2, 1975.

9 Postcard from A. I. Pushkin to the author dated May 2, 1969.

10 Conversation with A. P. Bor on June 20, 1995.

CHAPTER 4

1 Letter from G. P. Ianson to the author dated October 22, 1976.

2 Letter from J. Barker to K. I. Yurgenson dated April 3, 1970. A. I. Pushkin personal archive.

3 Letter from J. Barker dated March 14, 1968. A. I. Pushkin personal archive.

4 Conversation with M. M. Mikhailov on October 21, 1977.

5 Conversation with N. A. Dolgushin on January 30, 1973.

6 Ibid.

7 K. Goleizovskii, "Vladimir Viktorovich Vasil'ev," *Sovetskii artist* [Soviet Artist], No. 18 (1969): 3.

8 V. Krasovskaia, "Mikhail Baryshnikov's Concert," *Peterburgskii teatral'nyi zhurnal* [Petersburg Theater Journal], No. 1 (1993): 32.

9   Conversation with M. M. Mikhailov on October 21, 1977.

10   L. Lavrovskii, "Continuity of Traditions," *Vechernii Leningrad*, October 18, 1963, p. 4.

11   V. Kostrovitskaia and A. Pisarev, *Shkola klassicheskogo tantsa*. 1968. Trans. by John Barker as *School of Classical Dance* (London, 1995).

12   Notes to the discussion of the book by V. Kostrovitskaia and A. Pisarev. A. I. Pushkin personal archive.

13   TsGALI, St. Petersburg, f. 4462, op. 7, art. 40, p. 49.

14   Agrippina Vaganova, *Osnovy klassicheskogo tantsa*. 1934. Trans. by Anatole Chujoy as *Basic Principles of Classical Ballet* (London, 1953; repr. New York, 1969), p. 13.

15   Conversation with M. M. Mikhailov on October 21, 1977.

16   From "Dialogues." In: *Muzyka i khoreografiia sovremennogo baleta* [Music and Choreography in Contemporary Ballet] (Leningrad, 1974), p. 42.

17   Letter from G. P. Ianson to the author dated October 22, 1976.

18   Vaganova, *Basic Principles of Classical Ballet*, p. 135.

19   Transcript of the teachers' council of the Leningrad Choreographic School. TsGALI, St. Petersburg, f. 4464, op. 6, art. 143, p. 73.

20   Transcript of the teachers' council of the Leningrad Choreographic School. TsGALI, St. Petersburg, f. 4462, op. 7, art. 16, pp. 36–37.

21   TsGALI, St. Petersburg, f. 4462, op. 7, art. 31, p. 26.

22   A. I. Pushkin personal archive.

23   Vaganova, *Basic Principles of Classical Ballet*, p. 12.

24   Asaf Messerer, *Uroki klassicheskogo tantsa*. 1967. Trans. by Oleg Briansky as *Classes in Classical Ballet* (New York, 1975), p. 23.

25   V. D. Tikhomirov. *Artist, baletmeister, pedagog* [V. D. Tikhomirov. Artist, Ballet Master, Pedagogue] (Moscow, 1971).

26   Messerer, *Classes in Classical Ballet*, p. 23.

27   Conversation with M. M. Mikhailov on October 21, 1977.

28   A. Ia. Vaganova, "Paths of the Ballet." In: *A. Ia. Vaganova. Stat'i. Vospominaniia. Materialy* [A. Ia. Vaganova. Articles, Reminiscences, Materials] (Leningrad and Moscow, 1958), p. 65.

29   Karsavina, *Theatre Street*, p. 135.

Appendix: A. I. Pushkin's Classes

The combinations are given for the most part without indication of music.
All movements begin with the right leg.
All combinations are performed from both legs.

Senior Class *Late 1930s–Early 1940s*

Exercise at the Barre

1. Plié.
Two grands pliés each in first, second, fourth, and fifth positions.

2. Battements tendus and battements jetés.
Fifth position. Three battements tendus forward, three of them in demi-plié and half turn to barre en dedans. Right hand on barre, left in second position. Right foot back, repeat exercise. Half turn en dehors, eight battements tendus to the side in fifth position—the first time without changing position (right foot forward). Repeat entire combination in the reverse direction.

Four battements jetés forward, to the side, back, to the side. And sixteen (for each eighth) battements jetés in each position to the side.

3. Ronds de jambes par terre.
Three ronds de jambes par terre en dehors, the third through demi-plié. Repeat, but on the third time a grand rond de jambe jeté. Repeat entire combination en dedans.

6th port de bras, end in attitude effacée on half-toe.

4. Battements fondus.
One battement fondu forward, one to the side, demi-plié, leg raised 45 degrees. One tour en dedans, end turn in pose attitude effacée. Repeat entire combination in the reverse direction.

5. Ronds de jambes en l'air.
Two simple ronds de jambes, lower leg in fifth position. Two ronds de jambes en l'air with demi-plié and relevé, flic-flac en dehors. End to the side (leg at 45 degrees). Repeat entire combination in the reverse direction.

6. Adagio.
Développé forward, balancé, bring leg to the side, on the eighth return it forward and on the eighth bring it to the side. Lower right leg in fifth position behind left. Execute entire sequence in the reverse direction. Développé forward, bring leg behind. Demi-plié, fouetté in écartée and bring leg into 2nd arabesque on half-toe in effacée.

7. Battements frappés.
One battement double frappé to the front on demi-plié effacée, one to the side demi-plié, relevé (leg at 45 degrees). Seven battements frappés.

Three petits battements sur le cou-de-pied on the eighths—first time accent forward, repeat with accent back. End to the side pointe tendue. Two battements tendus pour batteries.

Repeat entire combination in the reverse direction.

8. Grands battements jetés.
Two grands battements jetés to the front in fifth position on the fourths and three grands battements jetés on the eighths. Then repeat everything to the side, the back, and again to the side.

Exercise in the Center

1. Petit Adagio.
Fifth position, right leg in front, croisée. Two pirouettes from fifth position en dehors, end in pose croisée front at 90 degrees, left arm in third position, right in second, change arms: right in third position, left in second. Grand rond to 4th arabesque to point 2, step on right foot to point 6 in pose attitude, left arm in third position, right in second. Tour lent to 1st arabesque to point 3, step with left leg to point 3, fouetté on left leg in 1st arabesque to point 7 (arms go through third position), close leg in fifth position croisée, right leg in front.

Four battements tendus front croisée on the fourths, three battements tendus jetés on the eighths, end in plié, two pirouettes from fifth position, end in fifth position croisée, right leg behind left. Repeat all en dedans. Repeat entire combination tendus once more.

2. Battements fondus.
Fifth position, right foot front, croisée. One battement fondu in écartée at 45 degrees to point 2, one fondu in écartée at 90 degrees, tombée to point 2 on right leg in pose 2nd arabesque, pas de bourrée in fourth position. Two pirouettes en dehors in pose attitude, end croisée in point 2 in plié, pas de bourrée en tournant en dehors, tombée to point 8 in fourth position, two pirouettes en dedans in 1st arabesque, end in 1st arabesque demi-plié and relevé in 1st arabesque.

3. Grands battements jetés.
Fifth position, right foot front, croisée. Préparation in second position. Two pirouettes en dehors, end croisée in pose attitude, plié, renversé, end in fifth position in beginning pose. Two grands battements forward croisée, two grands batte-

ments back croisée, four grands battements to the side en face. Repeat entire combination from the left leg.

4. Adagio.
Fifth position, right foot front, croisée. Grand plié in fifth position, one tour in 2nd arabesque, arms pass through preparatory position. End turn in plié in point 2 in 2nd arabesque, pas de bourrée en dehors, left foot in front, step with right to the side, fouetté with left effacée to effacée en dehors, end in pose allongée in point 2 at 90 degrees. Tour lent en dedans demi-plié to point 2, moving to half-toe in same position. Pas de ciseaux ending in 1st arabesque demi-plié to point 2; fouetté in écartée back, step on left to point 6, right through fifth position and through développé goes to pose écartée forward, tour lent en dedans to point 8, ending in pose attitude effacée, fouetté right leg effacée to effacée en dedans, pas de bourrée en dedans, ending in fifth position croisée.

Jumps

1. Fifth position, right leg behind croisée. One assemblé to the side, two changements de pieds, one assemblé to the side with the left, two changements de pieds (arms remain in preparatory position). One sissonne tombée forward croisée to point 2 with the left, assemblé back with the right, sissonne tombée with the right croisée to point 8 front, assemblé back with the left (arms for sissonne tombée: one in first position, the other in second, open position; at the assemblé the arms go to preparatory position). Repeat everything with the left forward, then execute the combination in the reverse direction.

2. Fifth position, right leg back croisée. One jeté to the side with right, temps levé (arms in jeté: right in first position, left

in second; in temps levé the position is retained). One jeté to the side with left (arms change), temps levé, right leg coupé, left assemblé to the side, end in fifth position, left leg in back. Two entrechat-quatre (arms in coupé-assemblé in preparatory position and retain position during lift). Repeat everything with left forward, then repeat entire combination in the reverse direction.

3. Fifth position, right foot behind croisée. Do brisé dessus-dessous twice, starting with the right, pas de bourrée en tournant en dehors, pas failli effacée to point 2, revoltade. Finish in 1st arabesque to point 2.

4. Fourth position, right foot in front croisée. Sissonne tombée en tournant à la seconde, assemblé with left, close in fifth position front. Sissonne tombée en tournant à la seconde, assemblé with right, close in front in fifth position. Two fermé with lift in 1st arabesque to point 2, sissonne failli in 4th arabesque, assemblé with right back to fifth position.

5. Fifth position, right foot in front. Sissonne tombée, cabriole in 1st arabesque to point 2, failli, sissonne cabriole fermée in 3rd arabesque to point 2, and twice tombée, coupé, jeté with croisée to croisée en tournant.

6. Fifth position, left foot in front. Glissade to the side with right, grand assemblé to the side, two entrechat-quatre, glissade to the side with left, grand assemblé to the side, two entrechat-quatre. Préparation in 1st arabesque on left foot to point 8, chassé back to point 4, sissonne fouetté attitude croisée, tombée effacée with left to point 8, pas de bourrée en dehors, double tour en l'air, end in fourth position croisée (right arm in third position, left in second).

7. Fifth position, left foot in front. Glissade, jeté in 1st

arabesque to point 2. Sissonne failli, cabriole fouetté in 1st position to point 7, sissonne failli with right to point 8, coupé, grand assemblé forward to point 8 (arms in assemblé in third position).

8. Fifth position, right foot in front. Échappé with lift to second position. From second position sissonne ouverte in attitude croisée to point 2. Assemblé with right back to fifth position, entrechat-six. Repeat another time. Then two times on half-toe perform entrechat-six and préparation to second position, pirouettes en dehors.

9. Port de bras.

Graduating Class *1967*

Exercise at the Barre

1. Plié.
Two grands pliés in each of the five positions.

2. Battements tendus and battements jetés.
Fifth position. One battement tendu, then one in demi-plié—execute the combination twice forward. To the side with pressure on the foot battement tendu in demi-plié two times. Repeat everything in the reverse direction.

Battement tendu to the side with pressure of the foot without demi-plié, two times, and four battements tendus without pressure. Repeat this combination two times. Battement jeté pointé forward two times, the third to the side, then three to the side and seven to the side in fifth position. Repeat everything in the reverse direction. Sixteen balançoires in first position and sixteen battements jetés in first position to the side. End on half-toe, right leg at 45 degrees. The arm is always in second position; at the end of the combination it is lowered (simultaneously with the leg) to the preparatory position.

3. Ronds de jambes par terre.
Two ronds de jambes par terre en dehors, the third in demi-plié. Two jetés passé, seven ronds de jambes par terre en dehors, and four grands ronds de jambes jetés. Repeat everything in the reverse direction. End in fifth position, right foot in front. Get on half-toe and execute 3rd form of port de bras. Dégagé with left to 4th arabesque, port de bras forward in this pose; passé with left and port de bras back. Demi-plié and turn en dehors (face the barre) to attitude effacée, left arm in third position.

4. Battements fondus.
One battement fondu forward at 45 degrees, lower leg onto toe, raise (dégagé) to 90 degrees. Repeat this combination to the side. Double fondu forward, demi-plié (leg at 45 degrees) and then rond de jambe (at 45 degrees) back. Fouetté en dehors (leg at 45 degrees), straighten supporting knee. Demi-plié and fouetté back to attitude effacée. Repeat everything in the reverse direction.

5. Ronds de jambes en l'air.
One rond de jambe en l'air plain, the second on demi-plié, three in a row, end on demi-plié. One tour (leg goes from second position at 45 degrees), two tours with temps relevé. Seven quick (on the eighths) ronds de jambes en l'air, flic-flac en dehors. End in pose écartée at 90 degrees. Repeat everything in the reverse direction.

6. Adagio.
Développé forward at 90 degrees in demi-plié, demi-rond to

the side, balance, passé, and rond de jambe, starting forward, ending back at 90 degrees. Tombée back, return to pose attitude (right arm in third position). Reverse rond de jambe at 90 degrees (right leg extended at the knee, and arm goes through first position to second position). Tombée forward, rise to fifth position on half-toe. Dégagé in 4th arabesque, demi-plié, half tour en dehors to pose attitude effacée (right hand on barre, left arm in third position). Passé with left and pose écartée back.

7. Battements frappés.
One battement double frappé forward, one back, battement double frappé with turn en dedans ending back (right foot lowers to toe, left in demi-plié). Repeat the combination, starting with right leg forward effacée (right hand on barre, left arm in second position). Two times three frappés to the side (on the eighths), five petits battements, and two tours with temps relevé. Repeat entire combination in the reverse direction.

8. Grands battements jetés.
One grand battement jeté forward, lower foot to the toe, the second in fifth position, the third also forward, soft, take foot through passé. Grand battement jeté with left behind. Seven balançoires (on the eighths) from movement forward, two to the side and two in pose écartée back. Repeat everything in the reverse direction.

Exercise in the Center

1. Adagio.
Grand plié in fifth position with port de bras and two tours (arms in third position). End turn in 3rd arabesque, turn en dehors, foot is moved forward through passé (arms allongée). Lower foot into fifth position. Sissonne, pas failli,

pose attitude on left leg, tour lent, full circle en dehors, up on half-toe in that pose and 6th form of port de bras. Préparation and tours en dedans sur le cou-de-pied with a stop in pose croisée forward, renversé into pose écartée to point 8, end in fourth position effacée. Two tours in pose 1st arabesque en dedans. Tour lent to pose 4th arabesque (straighten torso), renversé through passé to écartée back, pas failli in fourth position and two tours en dedans in pose attitude, bring foot through first position forward to fourth position and complete two tours en dehors in attitude, renversé, and pas de bourrée. End in fifth position. Without stopping: four battements tendus to the side, the fourth in demi-plié (arms change at the plié: one in first position, the other in third), seven battements jetés, end in fifth position, préparation, two pirouettes from second position, the préparation again, two pirouettes from second position. Repeat everything from the other leg.

2. Battements fondus.
Fifth position, right foot in front. One battement fondu in pose écartée forward 45 degrees, the second at 90 degrees, tombée effacée and two tours in attitude (right arm in third position, left in second). Arms through first position into second position, left foot to position à la seconde. Battement fondu to the side with the left foot at 45 degrees, demi-plié on right foot, fouetté in attitude effacée, pas de bourrée in fourth position (left foot in front), two tours à la seconde, demi-plié, transition in turning to pose attitude, which ends in pose effacée allongée. Failli, pas ciseaux in 1st arabesque, pas de bourrée in fourth position (right foot in front), two tours en dedans in 1st arabesque, demi-plié and fouetté on right to pose 3rd arabesque. Battement fondu in 3rd arabesque and fouetté en dehors to pose croisée forward at 90 degrees to point 2. Arms allongée, right in second position, left in third position.

3. Grands battements jetés.
Fifth position, right foot in front. Tours from second position, ending in pose attitude croisée, demi-plié, renversé pas de bourrée in fifth position on half-toe (left arm in third position, right in second). Balancé to the right and to the left, tombée effacée and two tours on right leg in 2nd arabesque, ending in demi-plié. Pas de bourrée in fourth position, two tours in pose croisée forward, end turn with fouetté in 2nd arabesque. Lower right leg forward into fifth position. Grands battements jetés on croisée forward two times (right arm in third position, left in second), two grands battements jetés in 3rd arabesque and two to the side with the right foot. Step with the left foot to the left, right brought through first position forward to préparation along the diagonal to point 2, two times soutenu, tombée effacée and two tours en dedans. Stop in 1st arabesque in demi-plié, bring left foot forward in fourth position and two tours en dehors, moving without stop into tours chaînés toward point 2. End in 1st arabesque in demi-plié (arms extended forward, right slightly higher than left).

4. Adagio.
Fifth position, right foot forward. Two times chassé, tombée, cabriole in 1st arabesque, two tours with demi-plié in 1st arabesque. Stop in attitude effacée, passé, développé front and come down to fourth position on left leg. Two tours in attitude en dehors, stop in 4th arabesque, pas de bourrée en tournant in fifth position. From second position, two tours à la seconde, two tours effacée, two tours in attitude, plié, pas de bourrée. End in fifth position.

5. Grand pirouette.

Jumps

1. Fifth position, left foot in front. Two assemblés (arms, changing during the jump, take the appropriate position: left in third position, right in second, and so on), third assemblé without the arms and entrechat-quatre. Two sissonnes fermées in pose écartée to point 2, sissonne ouverte in pose attitude to point 8, coupé with left leg behind right and assemblé with right leg forward. Repeat everything from the left foot.

2. Fifth position, left foot in front. Brisé forward, brisé back, four brisé en tournant en dedans (on the eighths). Two brisé forward and sissonne ouverte in attitude effacée on the right leg, pas de bourrée in fifth position. Sissonne tombée to the left, coupé with the right and assemblé with left leg with beat to the back. Repeat everything from the left leg.

3. Fifth position, left foot in front (combination begins with the right foot). Jeté, temps levé, renversé sauté, pas de bourrée in fifth position. Repeat everything. Jeté on right leg traveling to the side, left in front sur le cou-de-pied; jeté forward on left leg to point 2; right leg sur le cou-de-pied; brisé dessus-dessous. Step with right to effacée, tombée in pose allongée, jeté passé (flying pose). Fermé back with right to fifth position. Pas de basque from fifth to fifth position (right in front). Double sissonne ouverte en tournant to the side at 90 degrees. Assemblé with right foot in fifth position (back). Pause. Repeat combination from pas de basque in the reverse direction.

4. Fifth position, left foot in front. Glissade, cabriole fermé to the side, sissonne tombée, cabriole in 1st arabesque, failli, coupé, assemblé croisée forward (arms in third position), stand in fifth position on half-toe. Sissonne tombée effacée left, sissonne in 1st arabesque, pas chasée (traveling on diago-

nal to point 6), cabriole fouetté in 4th arabesque, sissonne tombée to the right (like the first time, but on the right foot) chassé and sissonne in position à la seconde, turn fouetté in jump to 1st arabesque, end on demi-plié.

5. Fifth position, right foot in front. Sissonne tombée on right leg, cabriole in 1st arabesque, failli, sissonne in pose attitude croisée on left leg, glissade to the right, cabriole fouetté in 1st arabesque, failli, sissonne in attitude croisée on right leg, glissade to the left, cabriole fouetté in 1st arabesque, failli and sissonne in pose attitude croisée on left leg. Sissonne tombée on right leg effacée to point 2, pas de bourrée in fifth position and two tours en l'air in fourth position.

6. Fifth position, left foot in front. Glissade, fouetté with beat in 1st arabesque, pas failli, cabriole in 4th arabesque. Repeat to the other side, ending in 4th arabesque. Tombée back and jeté en tournant, assemblé left leg in fifth position, entrechat-cinq. Jeté en tournant in attitude croisée to the other side, assemblé in fifth position and two tours en l'air in fourth position.

7. Fifth position, left foot in front. Glissade to the right, grand assemblé with beat to point 2. Stand in attitude croisée on right leg along the line of movement during assemblé. Repeat everything in the other direction. Tombée effacée with the left leg, ballonné with beat to the side and two times in a row jeté en tournant in attitude croisée. Run to the corner of the studio (point 6) and execute along the diagonal to point 2 sissonne tombée and grand jeté en tournant in attitude effacée, twice, two jetés en tournant (partner) and to the end of the musical phrase, tours chaînés.

8. Fifth position, right foot in front. Sissonne tombée on right leg in 1st arabesque and cabriole with beat forward in effacée

(right arm in third position, left in second). Repeat combination three times. Préparation in 1st arabesque and execute along the diagonal from point 2 to point 6 pas chassé and assemblé en tournant, tombée, pas de bourrée in fifth position and two tours en l'air. End in attitude croisée.

9. First and second parts of Albrecht's variation from Act II of *Giselle* (the last part is varied to accommodate student's abilities).

10. Siegfried's first coda from Act II of *Swan Lake*.

11. Assemblé en tournant in a circle.

12. Jeté en tournant in a circle.

13. Three entrechat-quatre, entrechat-trois—repeat this combination four times.

14. Port de bras.

Artists' Class *1960s*

Exercise at the Barre

1. Plié.
Two demi-pliés and one grand plié in first, second, fourth, and fifth positions. Right arm during the first demi-plié moves from second position and is lowered to preparatory position, during the second demi-plié from the preparatory position through first position to second. During the grand plié the right arm performs the same movement.

2. Battements tendus and battements jetés.
Fifth position. One battement tendu simple, second in plié—the combination to be done forward and to the side. Two battements tendus to the side with pressure of the foot without demi-plié and two battements tendus simple, to the side, the third in plié—repeat this combination two times. Then repeat everything in the reverse direction.

Two battements jetés forward (on the eighths), end the third in fifth position. Repeat the same exercise to the side. Seven balançoires through first position, beginning to the back. Repeat the entire combination in the reverse direction. Three battements jetés to the side (on the eighths) in fifth position—repeat the combination two times; and seven battements jetés in first position—repeat the combination two times.

3. Ronds de jambes par terre.
Three ronds de jambes par terre en dehors, the fourth in plié, bring the foot in demi-plié back along the floor, two jeté passé simple, the third ending in plié at 90 degrees, and four grands ronds de jambes jetés. Repeat everything in the reverse direction. End in fifth position, right foot in front. Développé with left leg in 4th arabesque, port de bras forward in this pose, passé with left and port de bras back. Open leg in pose attitude croisée, arms in third position. Fix this pose on half-toe.

4. Battements fondus.
One battement fondu forward 45 degrees, demi-plié and fouetté en dedans in pose attitude croisée (left arm in third position, right hand on the barre). Battement fondu with right leg (sur le cou-de-pied forward) 45 degrees, demi-plié and fouetté en dehors in attitude effacée. Two double fondus to the side, flic-flac en dehors, right leg open forward at 45

degrees and then rond de jambe to 2nd arabesque on half-toe. Repeat the entire combination in the reverse direction.

5. Ronds de jambes en l'air.
Two ronds de jambes en l'air, the third through demi-plié (on the eighths). Repeat three times. Demi-plié and one tour (from second position at 45 degrees), seven fast (on the eighths) ronds de jambes en l'air, the leg remains to the side at 45 degrees, two relevés and two tours (from second position at 45 degrees). Finish turn in attitude effacée at 90 degrees. Repeat the entire combination in the reverse direction.

6. Adagio.
Développé forward at 90 degrees, passé and développé to the side, rond de jambe back in demi-plié, relevé in attitude effacée allongée at 90 degrees on half-toe. Repeat everything in the reverse direction.

7. Battements frappés.
One battement double frappé forward, two pointés forward on the toe—execute the combination in all directions. Seven battements frappés to the side (on the eighths), seven battements jetés in fifth position to the side. End with right leg at 45 degrees to the side. Tombée on the right leg forward, left sur le cou-de-pied, stand on left leg and execute two tours with temps relevé. Repeat the combination in the reverse direction.

8. Grands battements jetés.
Two grands battements jetés forward, to the side, back, and to the side. Repeat the combination two times.

Exercise in the Center

1. Adagio.
Fifth position, right foot in front. Glissade to point 2 without changing legs, two tours from fifth position, end turn in pose effacée forward (right leg at 90 degrees to point 2). Step on right foot in 1st arabesque, tour lent en dedans to pose attitude croisée, sixth port de bras, and two tours en dedans. End turn in pose attitude effacée in demi-plié, pas de bourrée in fourth position (left foot forward). Two tours in attitude en dehors (on left foot), stop in demi-plié, renversé, pas de bourrée. End the combination in fifth position, right foot in front.

Two battements tendus to the side with the right foot (the first without changing feet in fifth position, that is, forward, the other back). Repeat in reverse. Seven battements jetés to the side in first position with the right foot, end in fifth position. Tombée in fourth position (right foot in front), two tours en dedans, ending turn in fourth position, left foot in front. Two tours en dehors, end in pose: right foot on toe in second position. Two times tours from second position. The entire combination is repeated, after a rest, from the other foot.

2. Battements fondus.
Fifth position, right foot in front. One fondu to the side at 45 degrees, the second in pose écartée at 90 degrees to point 4. Pas de bourrée in fourth position and grand pirouette in 1st arabesque, plié, tour in attitude, ending turn in pose allongée (left arm in third position). Bring left foot through fourth position forward, turn in pose croisée forward on left leg (en dedans); ending in 2nd arabesque to point 8 (right foot executes fouetté).

3. Grands battements jetés.
Two grands battements jetés in all poses: forward in croisée, to the side, back in arabesque, to the side. Immediately execute again from the other leg.

4. Turns (Adagio).
Fifth position, right foot forward. Tours from second position, ending in fourth position (right foot on the floor). Switch to right leg, left foot moves through first position back to pose attitude. Lower leg in fourth position in effacée and two tours à la seconde en dedans (arms in third position). Without stop: grand fouetté in 3rd arabesque. Lower left leg to fifth position. Rise on half-toe. Two pas chassé forward to point 8, tombée on right foot, two tours in attitude, tombée on left foot to point 2 and turn in pose attitude croisée (en dehors), demi-plié in this pose and move to turning en dehors (right foot in passé). End turn in 3rd arabesque.

Jumps

1. Fifth position, left foot in front. Three assemblés, first one leg, then the other to the side, entrechat-quatre. Assemblé with right forward, entrechat-quatre. Repeat with left leg to the back. Repeat the entire combination right away from the other leg.

2. Fifth position, left foot in front. Jeté, temps levé, jeté, temps levé. Ballonné with right leg to the side—repeat two more times to point 3. Assemblé back to fifth position. Pas de basque with left foot to point 8, double sissonne en tournant. Pas de basque with right foot to point 2 in double sissonne en tournant.

3. Fifth position, left foot in front. Glissade, cabriole fermée to point 2. The same combination to the other side, to point 8. Sissonne, cabriole in 1st arabesque on right leg along the diagonal to point 2, failli with left leg and sissonne on left leg (right leg in demi-attitude). Stand in 1st arabesque on right leg, step to point 6 and grand fouetté sauté in pose attitude croisée. Sissonne tombée, pas de bourrée to point 8, assemblé, two tours en l'air in pose attitude croisée.

4. Fifth position, left foot in front. Préparation: left foot on pointe in front on diagonal to point 2, right foot flat. Left arm in second position, right in first. Glissade to point 2 and grand jeté in 1st arabesque. Sissonne on right leg and pas couru with left traveling on the diagonal to point 2. Grand jeté on left leg to pose attitude croisée. Sissonne tombée on right leg and cabriole in 2nd arabesque. Step with left foot and pose 1st arabesque on right leg to point 2 on half-toe. From point 2 to point 6 two jetés entrelacés to 1st arabesque. Tours chaînés to point 2 and double sissonne en tournant. End on left knee effacée.

5. Fifth position, right foot in front (stand at point 7). Moving to point 3, make two sautés de basque in a row, get in 1st arabesque on right foot in half-toe. Pas de bourrée. End in fifth position. Repeat entire combination from left foot. Préparation on left and glissade to point 2, then double cabriole effacée front. Run to point 4 and execute two jetés en tournant along the diagonal to point 8 on right leg (back to point 1) in 4th arabesque. Tours chaînés. End in 3rd arabesque on right foot on the floor in point 8.

6. Fifth position, right foot in front: three entrechat-quatre, one entrechat-six. Repeat combination four times.

7. All forms of double tours en l'air: on diagonal to fourth position and 1st arabesque.

8. Port de bras.

About the Jerome Robbins Dance Division

The New York Public Library is one of the world's great libraries, providing leadership and standards for libraries everywhere. Established in 1895 by the consolidation of the private reference collections of John Jacob Astor and James Lenox with the Samuel Jones Tilden Trust, the Library now has collections that rival those of the world's foremost libraries and serve as one of the world's most extensive publicly accessible information resources. The New York Public Library operates four noncirculating research centers, which serve approximately two million people each year, and eighty-five circulating neighborhood branch libraries, which serve more than twelve million users annually.

One of the system's four research centers is The New York Public Library for the Performing Arts, located at Lincoln Center and housing the Jerome Robbins Dance Division. Including among its holdings the private collections of Lincoln Kirstein, Walter Toscanini, Agnes de Mille, Merce Cunningham, Rudolf Nureyev, and Jerome Robbins, among many others, it is the largest and most comprehensive archive in the world devoted to the documentation of dance. With a professional staff of dance specialists, it chronicles the art of dance in all its manifestations, providing information and multimedia documents about dance, old and new, as a daily free service. The division preserves the history of dance by gathering diverse written, visual, and aural resources. It works to ensure the art form's continuity through an active documentation program, videotaping dances and creating oral histories where adequate records do not exist. Founded in 1944 as a distinct unit of The Research Libraries of The New York Public Library, the Jerome Robbins Dance Division is used regularly by choreographers, dancers, critics, historians, journalists, publicists, filmmakers, videographers, graphic artists, students, and the general public. Working with the division's resources, a user can reconstruct an Elizabethan court dance, a nineteenth-century Italian tarantella, or a twentieth-century Ceylonese devil dance; determine what makeup Nijinsky wore in *Schéhérazade*; review Picasso's letters about the ballet *Parade*; or compare the modern dance styles of Isadora Duncan, Martha Graham, and Doris Humphrey. While the division contains more than 38,000 reference books about dance, these account for only 3 percent of its vast holdings. Other resources available for study include more than 16,000 films and videotapes (33,000 reels); 350,000 photographic prints and negatives; 30,000 files of newspaper clippings; 1,000 linear feet of manuscripts; 710 dance periodical titles from around the world, of which 210 are current subscriptions; 100,000 indexed magazine articles/reviews; 110,000 performance programs; 8,500 engravings and original scenic and costume designs; and nearly 4,000 hours of oral history.

This volume, *Alexander Pushkin: Master Teacher of Dance*, is one of a series of occasional publications produced by the Jerome Robbins Dance Division. The intent of this publication program is to supplement the activities of the commercial trade book industry and the scholarly presses. Additional avenues for making the division's holdings available to the public are regular exhibitions, loans of materials under appropriate conditions for special exhibitions in the United States and abroad, seminars and conferences, lectures and film screenings, instructional courses on dance research using electronic resources, and other public events.